D0437197

Wealthy by Design

A **5**-STEP PLAN FOR FINANCIAL SECURITY

Wealthy by Design

KIMBERLY FOSS, CFP©, CPWA©

FOUNDER OF EMPYRION WEALTH MANAGEMENT, INC.

GREENLEAF
BOOK GROUP PRESS

This publication is designed to provide accurate and authoritative information regarding the subject matter covered. It is sold with the understanding that the publisher and author are not engaged in rendering financial, legal, accounting, or other professional services. If expert assistance is required, the services of a competent professional should be sought. Some names and locations have been changed to protect identities, but all anecdotal stories are true and based on the author's personal experiences.

Published by Greenleaf Book Group Press
Austin, Texas
www.gbgpress.com

Copyright ©2013 Empyrion Wealth Management, Inc.

All rights reserved.

No part of this book may be reproduced, stored in a retrieval system, or transmitted by any means, electronic, mechanical, photocopying, recording, or otherwise, without written permission from the copyright holder.

Distributed by Greenleaf Book Group LLC

For ordering information or special discounts for bulk purchases, please contact Greenleaf Book Group LLC at PO Box 91869, Austin, TX 78709, 512.891.6100.

Design and composition by Greenleaf Book Group LLC
Cover design by Greenleaf Book Group LLC
Article on pages 12–13 reprinted with permission by *The Auburn Sentinel*.

Cataloging-in-Publication data
(Prepared by The Donohue Group, Inc.)

Foss, Kimberly.
 Wealthy by design : a 5-step plan for financial security / Kimberly Foss.—1st ed.
 p. ; cm.
 Issued also as an ebook.
 ISBN: 978-1-60832-573-3
 1. Investments. 2. Finance, Personal. 3. Wealth. I. Title.
HG4521 .F67 2013
332.67/8   2013934053

Part of the Tree Neutral® program, which offsets the number of trees consumed in the production and printing of this book by taking proactive steps, such as planting trees in direct proportion to the number of trees used:
www.treeneutral.com

TreeNeutral

Printed in the United States of America on acid-free paper

13 14 15 16 17 18   10 9 8 7 6 5 4 3 2 1

First Edition

This book is dedicated in loving memory to my parents, George and Gloria Foss, who inspired me and taught me the most important lesson in life: "Do the right thing first for all concerned, and the rest—including wealth—will follow."

I love and miss you both, and I will see you again soon.

CONTENTS

Introduction
October 10, 2008   1

STEP 1
Discovering and Setting Your Goals   9

STEP 2
Planning Your Investments   39

STEP 3
Committing to Your Plan   73

STEP 4
Assessing Your Plan   95

STEP 5
Keeping Your Plan Flexible   115

Conclusion
The Highest Reward   157

Acknowledgments   163

Appendix A
Questions to Ask a Prospective
Financial Advisor   165

Appendix B
Six Portfolio Allocation Strategies   171

Index   174

About the Author   181

OCTOBER 10, 2008

OCTOBER 10, 2008, is a day that's burned into my memory. Just as many people can tell you exactly where they were when they heard about JFK's assassination or when they first saw the images of the airliners hitting the Twin Towers on 9/11, I can clearly recall where I was and what I was doing on October 10, 2008.

The Dow plunged nearly 700 points that day to its lowest reading in more than five years. By the day's end, the Big Board had recovered, if one can use that word to describe closing down "only" 128 points. For the week, the Dow had lost almost 1,900 points, the worst decline, both in points and percentage of value, in the entire 112-year history of the exchange.

The stock market was reacting to a string of bankruptcies and forced reorganizations among some of the world's largest financial firms, calamities brought about in large part by the housing bubble burst in 2007 and the gridlock in credit markets that followed. Credit markets stalled due to lenders' fears of "toxic assets"—subprime mortgage loans packaged as securities and sold to institutional and private investors. As long as the housing boom kept going and home prices continued to climb, all was well. But when the day came—as such days always will—when enough people

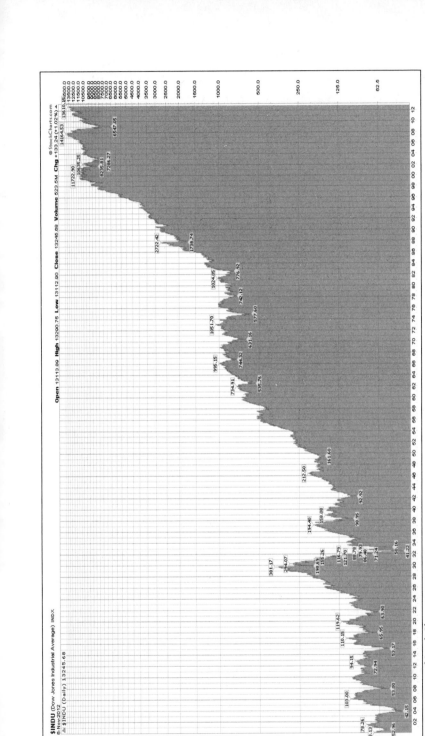

Chart courtesy of StockCharts.com

stopped making payments on loans they couldn't afford in the first place, foreclosures started to rise and home prices began to tumble. Now the stock market was following suit.

World finance ministers issued a statement warning that exceptional steps would be needed to ease the global financial crisis and to get the credit markets unfrozen. In an effort to maintain adequate liquidity so that a meltdown could be prevented, the Federal Reserve had already coordinated with central banks in other nations and announced an emergency rate cut. Despite these efforts, however, banks all over the world were hoarding cash, adding fuel to the fire as panicked investors watched a market in free-fall.

My first thoughts that day were of my family. How would I, a wife and mother of four, provide for my children when the financial world had fallen apart? Would my children ever have the same opportunities to achieve their dreams as I had? Would there be enough of an economy left for them—or for anyone—to make their way?

My second thoughts were of my clients. How would this financial disaster affect their portfolios, their security, and the rest of their lives? What could I do to protect them and to justify the trust they had placed in me?

As it turned out, I was able both to protect my clients and to help them turn handsome profits in their portfolios, despite the chaotic events of October 10, 2008, and the shaky markets that continued for some time thereafter. Along the way, I structured an investment that allowed my clients to participate in the rescue of Morgan Stanley, one of the world's largest banks, during the aftermath of the market panic—and to make some very attractive returns while doing so.

I could do these things because of the time-tested principles that I've learned over more than three decades helping people plan for and find financial security—the same principles that I'll share with you in this book. During my career, I have learned one central fact: it's not really about money. Instead, it's about people first, then profits. Family, schooling, and career history have as much to do with financial security as savings and income do. Because I realize that my own personal history played a large part in making my financial career what it is today, I have my clients examine their own lives as their first step toward achieving financial success.

What you will find in this book are interwoven stories, each of which may touch or compel you differently, depending on where you are coming from. This is the story of my life and of the skills I learned along the way that enabled me to become a successful financial advisor. It tells what I came to love (and hate) about the financial business, and how I managed to survive and even thrive during the financial crisis of 2008. Students planning a career in economics or wealth management will find personal inspiration as well as a few nuggets from the research literature that will spark their thinking when term paper or dissertation topics come due.

Financial professionals in the early or middle stages of their careers will learn that the steps I've mapped out in the five chapters of this book correspond to five distinct stages they can intentionally build into their relationships with clients. These are the five steps that I have distilled as best practices based on my thirty-plus years of experience in the field:

1. Discovery

2. Investment planning

3. Mutual commitment

4. Sixty-day follow-up assessment

5. Regular progress meetings to ensure the plan's flexibility

As you read, you'll see how these steps relate to my life cycle as a professional and also to the investment progression of my clients. I'll show you how I help my clients build a tangible plan for protecting and accumulating wealth to create a secure future for themselves, their loved ones, and the causes and people they believe in. I'll also illustrate how I help my clients make sure that their plan is working, as well as how to determine whether it requires some mid-course correction. Depending on the topics you already cover with your wealth management clients, you may choose to execute the above steps in a variety of ways, incorporating them into your routine as additional in-person meetings and other communications, or whatever combination serves you and your clients best.

My story follows a path to financial independence that anyone can take. That is to say, this book is also for investors. You may be engaged in hands-on self-education with your money, allowing a small amount each month to create your own wealth using Charles Schwab or Vanguard's do-it-yourself service, just to get a feel for how investment works. If you've now mastered the basics and are ready to move beyond what your experimentation, the Motley Fool, and the newspaper's business section can teach you, then this book will help you envision your next step.

If, on the other hand, you are already working with a wealth advisor and are seeking a higher level of service than what you are presently receiving, this book is also for you. It will provide you specific questions to ask as you interview other advisors about their services. While those investors who are ready to work with a financial professional are best placed to take advantage of the lessons in this book, I've made it a point to include resources for further reading that will help people who are not yet in a position to do so. We all have goals, dreams, financial needs, and desires, after all.

You may get a glimpse of yourself, or of someone you hope to one day be, in the case studies of clients I've included in this book.

While each case study is fictionalized to protect client privacy and while many combine aspects of different clients, they illustrate the general characteristics of people I've been able to help:

- Gen Xers and Yers: twenty- and thirty-somethings who need help making wise financial decisions, or who are in need of financial counsel due to sudden wealth from inheritance money;
- 'Tweeners: forty-five- to sixty-year-olds who are approaching, but not at, retirement age and who have amassed savings from which they want to reap maximum benefits while exploring a second career;
- Women in transition: widows, divorcees, or successful business owners who've sold their businesses, each of whom needs assistance in transitioning her assets to the next chapter of her life; and
- Pre- and post-retirees: people who have spent a lifetime building up their wealth and who now need to know how to maximize their return on investment while minimizing the chance that they will outlive their money.

By looking at these examples and seeing how I was able to help each one move through the five steps to financial success, you'll gain practical insights that you can apply to your own financial situation. No matter where you are on the spectrum of investment experience, my aim is to equip you with the tools you need to become a smart consumer of financial services.

Despite the rampant greed and cynicism that almost brought the financial markets to their knees in October 2008, I truly believe that hope and opportunity are still what this country is built on. The American capitalist system allowed me to aim high, work hard, and achieve my dreams, and it can do the same for you, too. That's why, as I sat in my office on October 10, 2008, and stared into the looming abyss of worldwide financial collapse, I could not abandon hope. As author John Maxwell has said, "Where there is no hope in the future, there is no power in the present." My clients had trusted me with their hopes and dreams, represented by their hard-earned investments. I knew there had to be a way for me to protect those dreams, as well as the futures I had so carefully helped them plan. And because of the principles explained in this book, I was successful.

But to find the roots of my success, I must return to when I was a kid, growing up in a crowded home in a small town in Northern California, dreaming of a different kind of life.

DISCOVERING AND SETTING YOUR GOALS

GOALS TRANSFORM WISHES into plans. The moment you set a firm goal and decide that it's something you're willing to take action to achieve, you have taken the first crucial step in transforming that wish into a reality.

In my financial advising practice, I've been privileged to assist people not only in achieving their financial objectives, but also in formulating the life goals that provide the motivation to build and maintain wealth in the first place. As I said, it's really not about the money—it's about the choices that the money can provide. And those choices are determined in large part by your life experiences, by your inclinations and desires, and sometimes even by the things you've learned to dislike.

THE EARLY YEARS OF A FINANCIAL ADVISOR

Some people have the idea that those of us in the financial professions have been around money all our lives. Maybe you've envisioned the story: we grow up swimming in the country club pool, vacationing in the Caribbean and Europe, going to school at places where a pedigree is one of the admission requirements. Then, after completing our obligatory four years at an Ivy League school, we hang out our stockbroker's shingle and settle in to a life of golf, parties, and investing trust funds for our parents and their friends.

I can guarantee you that my life, at least, bears no resemblance to that rosy picture. My father was a carpenter—a blue-collar, hardworking man with an eighth-grade education who, in his whole life, never made more than $22,000 in a single year. My mother was the ever-charismatic Avon lady from whom you bought products even though you didn't need them—yes, she was that good, and a very intelligent woman as well. There were six children in the house, and I was the youngest. My oldest sibling was nearly twenty when I was born. Needless to say, I was never the first one to wear a pair of jeans, let alone anything with a designer label—at least until I was old enough to earn my own money. I lived in hand-me-downs.

I've done a lot of thinking about what it means to grow up in humble circumstances. I think people in that situation can go one of two ways: either they never imagine anything different for themselves, eventually coming to accept that this sort of life is all that's available to them; or they somehow catch the desire for something more—they strive to live a different kind of life.

There was one thing that my parents gave me in abundance: the power to dream. When it came to imagining what I could be when I grew up, they gave me carte blanche. In fact, the future became the ultimate fantasy world for my young, creative mind. I felt that I could achieve anything I set my mind to. The message from my parents was always, "Kimberly, if you believe it, you can do it." And because they believed it, I believed it too.

What I really believed in—what I really desired—was a different lifestyle. I didn't want to be trapped by the circumstances of my birth. When I was young, if our car broke down and we couldn't get a ride from a friend or a neighbor, we couldn't get anywhere. To me, it seemed that we were constantly trapped. I would ask myself, "Why does it have to be like this? Why do we have to live this way?"

We must all have been dissatisfied with our circumstances, but for some reason, I felt that it affected me more than it did my siblings. It was impossible for me to become comfortable with the idea of accepting those circumstances; I had a special kind of determination to turn those dreams my parents encouraged me to have into actual goals. Maybe my determination had something to do with the place we lived in.

I was born in Auburn, California, a little town nestled at the base of the foothills on Interstate 80. Auburn was founded in 1849, during the gold rush. The people who settled there were driven by the desire to succeed, to have more. It was a hard and dangerous life, but the people who lived in the area had grit and determination.

One of those people was my great-great-grandfather Daniel Austin Rice, the first Wells Fargo agent in the greater Sacramento Valley in Northern California. As the story goes, he was responsible for transporting gold from Rattlesnake Bar, near Auburn, to Sutter's Fort in Sacramento, where the bank held the gold for safekeeping.

Unfortunately, there was a notorious bank robber named Rattlesnake Dick, a ruthless man with a nasty reputation for robbing stagecoaches. According to the stories I heard growing up, my great-great-grandfather, after being robbed several times by Rattlesnake Dick, searched him out and used his famous charisma (the same charm for making sales my mother obviously inherited) to start a negotiation with the outlaw, and actually struck a deal with him, agreeing to leave Dick a small payoff if he would leave the stagecoach alone during his run.

Great-great-Grandpa Rice's granddaughter was my grandmother. Edna Evangeline Rice was a deeply religious and faithful woman. She possessed the patience of Job and waited until her mid-thirties

Auburn, California   April 2, 1993   Vol. 4, No. 13

A TOWN CALLED RATTLESNAKE by Bill Wilson

When Daniel Austin Rice settled in the office as the first Wells, Fargo & Company agent in Rattlesnake in the early 1857, he could look out and see a boisterous gold-mining river town—a town that lived fast but died young.

He probably was in the audience to hear the noted singer Kate Hayes belt out "Then You Will Remember Me" in the theater building shortly after he arrived in town. Each day he also could not get it out of his mind that highwayman Richard Barter, known as the dreaded "Rattlesnake Dick," might hit one of the stages heading away from his office on the way to Auburn or Sacramento.

"There was the story that a sack containing gold would be left on a designated rock near the town for the highwayman," James Edmund Rice, his son and also a Wells Fargo agent, told his granddaughter Gloria Foss before he died. "It apparently was easier to leave the money so he wouldn't rob the stage," was the way Rice explained the payoff.

"I don't know if that was true," said Foss, a resident of Auburn since 1950, "but the story was told time after time."

There were some 1,500 people living at Rattlesnake, located some six miles south of Auburn on the American River, when the senior Rice took over the Wells Fargo office in 1857. Barter was living there at the time and had come to the attention of law enforcement officials when he was accused of stealing some goods from a Jewish merchant and running off with a miner's mule.

The senior Rice had taken over the Wells Fargo office four years after John C. Barnett uncovered one of the richest discoveries of gold along the American River while he was prospecting on a flat ledge at the town site on May 7, 1853. It was reported that when he and his hired hands reached bedrock some 20 feet below the surface soil the first pan sifted contained $15 in gold. The next netted $20, and the rush was on.

Rattlesnake blossomed, and soon it became the principal town along the river where miners rushed to get to by foot, horseback and mule, all dreaming they would find a fortune. Within days, Frank Brown organized a daily stage to and from Sacramento, and within two months the Bear River Ditch Company supplied water to the mine.

The legendary driver Hank Monk drove to and from the town during its hey-day, and Moses Andrews, who later became a successful banker and businessman in Auburn, was justice of the peace. Thomas Woods took over as postmaster when the post office was established there in December 1854. Early the next year a wagon road on the El Dorado side of the river was completed, and the Whiskey Bar wire suspension bridge was erected to connect the town with the many rich river gravel bars and mines on the south side.

A theater was constructed and the Wells Fargo office was opened and Rice and his wife, Marian Forbes Rice, settled in the town to raise their family. The couple had migrated west from Massachusetts.

The Rattlesnake Theater, and the free-spending miners, lured a number of gold mining entertaining stars to the town, and when Hayes arrived there it turned into a wild celebration. When she closed her program with "Home, Sweet Home," teary-eyed homesick miners bombarded the stage with nuggets and coins.

Barter, who had come to Rattlesnake to search for gold, knew Hayes and met her after the show, according to news accounts. His freedom to be with the noted singer, however, was short-lived, and the next day he was arrested for a minor offense and taken to Auburn and lodged in the county jail. Barter escaped from the jail and fled the county to begin a series of stage robberies that made him one of the most sought after criminal offenders in the state.

Two years later, Hayes returned to Rattlesnake to sing again and Barter, now known widely as "Rattlesnake Dick," was there to hear her. He was recognized there, the story goes, and he was arrested again only to escape from custody. It is not known if he ever saw Hayes again, for two years later he was shot to death by law enforcement officers near Auburn.

During the late 1850s, the mining town continued to explode with people when miners working the gravel bars rendezvoused in the saloons and other businesses to relate of their success. Some were telling of recovering $150 in gold from each pan, and the Wells Fargo office and Rice continued to ship large amounts of the precious metal to financial houses in Sacramento and San Francisco.

As long as gold was being found along the many bars and other canyon mines, Rattlesnake flourished. In 1857, there were more than 300 votes cast in the town out of the 4,219 in the county when Joseph Walkup of Auburn was elected California lieutenant governor and a majority of the local voters approved the holding of a convention to revise the State Constitution.

Daniel Austin Rice was the first Wells, Fargo & Company agent in the mining town of Rattlesnake on the American River.

Marian Forbes Rice, wife of Daniel A. Rice, was one of the few women living in the town of Rattlesnake in 1857.

The town of Rattlesnake was an open frontier town, and it had its brutal murders, gun and knife play, along with its fights and confrontations. One of the incidents that shocked its residents was on June 3, 1856, when Phineas A. Longley, a toll keeper on the Whiskey Bar Bridge, was murdered at his post. The suspects were a party of renegade Indians.

Justice was quick at times, but sometimes offenses against neighbors were treated with understanding and compassion. Such was the case during the early days of Rattlesnake when Judge J.M. Frey heard a complaint of assault and battery with "attempt to kill" against Henry Himmerman. A witness for the prosecution testified that Himmerman threw a boot at clothing store owner John Friday.

The court reported that "the sympathies of the people were decidedly with the defendant because he had a wife and two small children to support." Himmerman was ordered to pay court costs, some four dollars.

But Himmerman did not get off without an admonishment. Judge Frey warned him that if he ever threw a boot at Mr. Friday again, "I will be compelled to move you out of your family setting and have you take lodging with Sheriff Astin in Auburn."

A fire that swept through the town on October 7, 1863, destroyed seven of the main buildings, including the theater and hotel. Although Rattlesnake had started on the decline, the fire was the death knell for the town. In the early 1860s many of its residents had begun moving to Newcastle, Auburn and the Penryn area.

Rice took his family and moved to Newcastle where his son, James, became an agent for Wells

James Edmund Rice, son of Daniel and Marian Rice and who was born in Rattlesnake, followed in his father's footsteps by becoming a Wells, Fargo & Company agent.

The official appointment of Daniel Austin Rice as Wells, Fargo & Company agent in the town of Rattlesnake remains in the possession of Rice's great-granddaughter, Gloria Foss of Auburn.

Daniel A. Rice (left) and his brother, James, stand in front of the Wells, Fargo & Company office in Newcastle. James was the company agent in Newcastle.

Fargo. The younger Rice also took Wells Fargo assignments in Stockton and other Central Valley towns. He and his wife, Alice Berry Rice, lived their final years in Auburn.

The Rice family, like many pioneer families who first settled in the river mining town of Rattlesnake, were unlike the town that lived fast and died before adulthood. The families survived and generation after generation continued in the traditions of the men who came and conquered.

to marry her soul mate in order to be sure she would be financially secure in an otherwise uncertain economic time. My grandfather, Dr. Glover Brown Wilcox, was a surgeon and doctor in San Francisco. He graduated from medical school at USC and served in the Great War (or World War I, as it is presently referred to) as a first lieutenant in the Medical Service Corps in the United States Army in 1917. After the war's end, my grandfather began a successful practice in San Francisco. However, as fate would have it, he passed away while attending to his patients in 1922. He contracted pneumonia from a house-call patient and never recovered, only a year after my mother was born. My grandmother was suddenly a single parent. She never remarried, and continued to raise my mother in San Francisco, solo. In those times, because my grandmother was a doctor's widow, they might have been considered "high society," but like everyone else during those difficult times, they struggled to make ends meet, especially during the Great Depression, following the collapse of the stock market in 1929.

At times, I felt that I didn't belong with the rest of my family. I was the only one who cared about money. I wasn't greedy, although my siblings joked endlessly that I loved the greenback more than my family, but it did seem as if my brothers and sisters didn't see money the way I did. They saw it more as a means of getting by, or as an occasional treat, whereas I saw it as an opportunity for choice. I saw that money allowed a person options in life, freedom from feeling trapped and from living paycheck to paycheck. Because of these differences, I felt isolated, like the black sheep of the family.

That is, until the day (I think I was not even ten years old) when my mother told me, "You know, you're just like your great-great-grandfather and my father, Kimberly."

I asked, "Why?"

She said, "Both your great-great-grandfather and grandfather were very intelligent, intuitive, and had an incredibly astute business sense that complemented their God-given gifts; but they also knew how to attract quality people and how to help them fully develop their unique gifts, as well. This allowed both your ancestors to leverage their respective time and create an impactful and meaningful legacy to improve the lives of all those whom they touched while they were on this earth. You, my youngest one, possess those same qualities. Kimberly, God has blessed you with the best of your father's gifts and the best of mine, and in turn, I believe you're destined to do great things in your life."

I remember thinking, *Wow! I do fit into this family, after all!* All the pieces of my family history fell effortlessly into place. All the dots now connected, from my great-great-grandfather's career with Wells Fargo during the gold rush to my grandfather's ability to multitask a successful medical practice in San Francisco and save people's lives at the risk of his own: I fit in. To this day, my mother's words and the message she instilled in me at that tender age have never left me and are a source of daily inspiration.

I GREW UP in a loving, supportive home, and I adore my family to this day. I just saw certain things differently than they did. As a child, I couldn't quite make the connection between success and attracting quality people that I could help, like my grandfather had done. Regardless, I always kept the same image in my mind: the white picket fence, the manicured lawn, the late-model car in the driveway. Those differences between us determined the goals I began to set for myself.

For example, as a teenager, I really wanted a pair of jeans—brand new ones, ones that hadn't already been worn by several of my older sisters. Jordache jeans were the "in" item at that time, and they cost $35 a pair. For my family, that might as well have been $10,000. But I desperately wanted a pair, so I asked my mother.

"Jordache jeans?" she said. "We can't afford those!"

"If I make the money myself, may I buy them?" I asked.

"Sure," she said, "if you earn the money and put half away for savings, you can do whatever you want with the remainder."

At that point, my mother was so busy that she probably didn't even know what she was agreeing to. I could have said, "Mother, can I go play on the highway?" and she'd say, "Yeah, fine, great." (Today's busy moms reading this can relate, I'm sure.) But regardless of the circumstances, I'd gotten her approval. Now I just needed a way to get the money for my jeans.

The upper part of our half-acre lot was occupied by our home, and the rest contained blackberry bushes that were perpetually full of scraps from dad's carpentry work. The mess embarrassed me, so I asked my father for a job. I would cut down the berry bushes with a sickle, haul all of the thorn-covered vines to the junk pile, and then build a rock wall where the bushes had been. He agreed to pay me the exorbitant sum of a dollar an hour. I worked steadily until I had enough money to go down to the store and buy my Jordache jeans. I continued to work until the project was complete, and that resulted in enough money to stash away in my blue combination strongbox, the beginnings of a college fund and a "rainy day fund"—today's emergency fund. I still have those jeans today.

Somewhere around age eleven, I decided that my next goal would be to go to college. A degree was going to be my road to more money, which meant more choices. It was going to be my path toward my personal utopia.

To further that goal, I became my father's "assistant" and helped him to hang sheetrock, lay title, pour concrete—whatever he needed me to assist with, I was there. That also developed a strong work ethic and connected the capitalistic dots, as it were, for me for the first time. I saved all the money I could in that blue strongbox.

When I turned seventeen, the first Long's Drugs (now CVS Pharmacy) opened in Auburn. They were looking for young people to hire. I remember being nervous about the required arithmetic test, but I passed it and was hired. Within about two months, the Long's Drugs management promoted me to the cosmetics department. I attribute this to my flair for fashion, of course, but mainly to my strong work ethic, instilled by hauling thorny vines and hanging sheetrock for my father.

In my senior year of high school, I started working full time (forty hours a week) for the store. I had taken almost enough classes to graduate and the only requirements I had left were senior English and civics. Still, even with the reduced course load, it wasn't easy to balance a full work schedule with school and everything else in my life. But it was worth it. I knew I needed to earn enough money for college, because my mother and father had no money to spare for such "luxuries."

I graduated on schedule in June 1980 and attended Sierra Junior College for my freshman year. That let me live at home and keep my full-time job while I raised additional funds for college. And it worked: combined with college grants, a Masonic scholarship, some savings, and a few student loans, that job brought in just enough to fund the college of my choice, where I earned a degree in business with a minor in computer science in three and a half years.

In the end, achieving my college goals wasn't much different from buying the Jordache jeans. I knew what I wanted. I knew that it would take a certain amount of money to give me the choice to pursue what I wanted. And no matter how difficult the doing got to be, I decided to do it. Setting goals was the first step on the path that allowed me to build the life I wanted—which was far from the circumstances into which I was born.

THE IMPORTANCE OF GOALS

As you read my story and think about your own experiences, keep in mind the idea that family background is very important in determining the goals we set and—even more important—in how we'll instinctively seek to achieve these goals.

In my case, growing up in a home where money was always tight spurred me to set goals that would point me toward a life that afforded me the choices that wealth can provide. My parents consistently modeled the value of hard work and always encouraged me to have big dreams and challenging objectives, but the lifestyle they provided wasn't what I had envisioned for myself, and that heavily influenced my behavior when it came to long-term planning. By the time I was eleven, I had set goals that included college, a professional career, and a very different life trajectory than that of my parents.

Our families have an influence on our financial behavior. For example, imagine you had a father who was a saver—he never spent a dime that he didn't have to. Depending on how you felt about his behavior, you'd either decide to do the same, or maybe you'd decide you hated having to make do with broken or substandard appliances or out-of-fashion clothes when you technically had the money available in savings to do something about it. In other words, whether you were aware of it or not, you'd develop a positive or a negative attitude toward saving money versus spending it, and that attitude would necessarily influence your financial behavior once you got out on your own. Or, conversely, imagine you had a parent who always bought the latest gadgets, the newest fashions, the most expensive cars—and who perhaps struggled to find money for more important long-term purposes. You may have observed that and determined, whether consciously or not, that this was the right way to behave—or that you would never spend money on luxuries until the necessities were taken care of.

So why do people from the same family sometimes have such different reactions to the financial behavior of their parents? From a study begun in Sweden in 2008 of 15,000 different sets of identical and fraternal twins, we know that many of our financial tendencies have a genetic origin.[1] Environment and experience clearly play a large part as well, but the findings of the study indicate that by the time we reach our forties, most of our financial behavior is shaped by our genetic makeup rather than by what we've observed or learned from our parents and others. In other words, a certain proportion of the population consists of innate spenders, while others are innate savers. Short of rewiring one's genetic code, there's nothing anyone can do about changing that inborn nature.

As a financial advisor, I've learned that when a client is an innate spender, the best practice is to get them to recognize their tendencies so that we can set up mechanisms to help them avoid overspending. I work *with* their natural tendencies rather than against them to help meet the goals that we've established together.

Case Study: Jake (Gen Xer)

I remember when Jake first came to see me. Jake was privileged to have grandparents who had been saving for his education since he was born. As he prepared to enter graduate school in New York City, he realized that he needed financial advice and guidance to provide the best possible stewardship of the gift he had been given. With the funds from his grandparents, Jake had financial assets in the neighborhood of a million dollars, quite a sobering responsibility for a young person.

Add to that the fact that Jake had a tendency to be a spender; he shared this honest self-assessment with me very early in our

---

1. Henrik Cronqvist and Stephan Siegel, "The Origins of Savings Behavior," AFA Denver Meetings Paper 2011, available online at http://papers.ssrn.com/sol3/papers.cfm?abstract_id=1649790.

time together. For these and other reasons, Jake was eager to gain the assistance of someone who could help him make sense of the world of investing, a "financial coach" who could help him form some good habits that would serve him well for the rest of his life.

Jake took his responsibilities toward his grandparents' generosity very seriously, so he made it clear that his goals included making wise use of his opportunities. He wanted to concentrate on his studies and eventually to seek a career in the nonprofit sector based upon his personal satisfaction rather than on the size of his salary. He also wanted to maintain a certain lifestyle, to travel and perhaps to purchase a home after he finished graduate school.

Jake's goals, dreams, and objectives informed the investment strategies he ultimately chose—strategies that would provide for security of principal with conservative growth characteristics. But given his innate financial behavior, it was also important to help him stay on track toward meeting his goals by putting some month-to-month disciplines and budgeting in place as barriers to the kind of unconsidered spending that would compromise his future financial security.

To establish those barriers, I had Jake set up a profile with the website Mint.com. Mint.com is an easy-to-use, interactive financial tool and is one of the best ways I've found to help clients organize their finances, understand where their money is going each month, and develop a strategic view of how all their financial assets are working together to move them toward their goals. Getting Jake in the habit of establishing financial discipline for himself helped him to understand and work with his innate "spender" tendencies, which allowed him to direct his assets toward achieving his goals.

Jake was eager to gain the assistance of someone who could help him make sense of the world of investing, a "financial coach" who could help him form some good habits that would serve him well for the rest of his life.

WHO CAN ANSWER MY QUESTIONS?

This is probably the most important thing you can ask yourself when you begin to think about your overall wealth goals in a systematic way. After all, your plan is only as good as the information on which it is based, and your assessment process (which we'll talk about in a later chapter) will only be as good as the ongoing guidance and information that you receive. If you choose to work with a financial advisor, it is essential, especially in the turbulent markets since 2008, that you find one upon whom you can depend: one who has your best interests (not the commissions he or she will receive by trading in your account) at heart.

Given the volatility of today's markets, the reprehensible acts of some of the world's financial giants, and the burgeoning domestic and international debt loads, I firmly believe that the first step to getting serious as an investor is to find an experienced, ethical, morally dedicated advisor. Today's financial markets can often resemble a raging white-water torrent rushing between the rock walls of a canyon. I would not try to get in that treacherous river without an experienced guide at my back. There has never been a time when good advice was more valuable than it is today.

Twenty years ago if you had, say, $10,000 to $500,000 of investable assets, I might have recommended simply getting some good books to learn investment principles and sent you on your way; these days I advise anyone with *any amount* of investable assets to find the best advice you can get for your dollar, whether that's a book, a seminar, or a wealth advisor. In the next chapter, I'll provide some more details about how to find the best, most personal financial advice you can afford.

The fact is that you can only afford to make the wrong choice a couple of times at most, and maybe even just once. If you're young and your investments start to go in the wrong direction, you've got time to recover. You won't enjoy it, but it is possible. But for people who are into their retirement years, the stakes are much higher. If they make a misstep and suffer a significant loss of their asset value, they don't have as much time to recoup their losses.

Choosing the right financial advisor is perhaps the most important thing you can do to ensure that you don't take that misstep. A recent major survey of affluent investors showed that 90.2 percent of them were inclined to work with financial advisors.[2] Choosing the right advisor is the key to the success of your financial plan, and you need to find someone with whom you can build a strong relationship based on honest communication, integrity, and trust. You owe it to yourself as an investor to ensure that your investment plan is constructed to withstand the stresses of the markets.

In a complex world where there are so many demands on our attention, it is impossible to be good at everything. As I'll stress later in the book, most of us are not good at remaining logical and cool under pressure when it comes to our investment decisions. Therein lies the value of working with a qualified financial advisor who can help you design a plan to meet your goals, who will commit to your financial welfare, and who will work with you on

---

2. Larry Barrett, "Advisors Really Do Offer Value: Survey," *Financial Planning*, 16 July 2012, www.financial-planning.com/news/limra-survey-importance -effectiveness-financial-advisors-clients-2679840-1.html.

an ongoing, systematic basis to assess your progress and help keep you on course.

Here are some of the questions that clients typically ask me when considering using me as their financial advisor:

Q: Kimberly, how do you get paid for managing my investments?

A: I am a "fee-only" advisor. I am compensated on a flat fee that is a percentage of the value of the assets I manage for you. If your assets go up in value, my fee does as well; if they go down, my fee decreases too. These fees are based on the assets under management, or AUM. (I'll discuss why I work on a fee basis in a later chapter.)

Q: How will I get my [monthly, quarterly, annual] income checks from my account?

A: In addition to the monthly statements provided by Charles Schwab (the custodian we clear through), I provide you with custom quarterly reports that list your investments along with the annual and monthly income generated by those investments. I provide a clear explanation of how the account will pay the income, the frequency with which interest and dividends will be received, and the amount of investment income you can expect from your overall portfolio design (the "drip" that I'll discuss later in the book).

Q: Why do you use the Dimensional Fund Advisors mutual funds?

A: I have access to the full range of Dimensional Fund Advisors mutual funds, which are only available to institutional investors and other approved advisors. Due to the extremely low expense costs to run these funds, they typically run well below the costs that most retail investors would otherwise pay. With the access to the Dimensional Fund Advisors low-cost funds, I am able to create a balanced investment portfolio for about $0.40 per every $100 invested into the fund (the typical no-load, self-managed portfolio

Current Income Estimate Report

Security	Market Value	Estimated Annual Yield	Frequency	Total Est. Gross Annual Income	
Bank of Nova Scotia	18,099.62	3.94%	Q	713.13	
Conoco Phillips	28,313.05	3.40%	Q	962.64	
Google Inc.	31,674.50		Q		
Kraft Foods Inc.	19,175.00	3.30%	Q	632.78	
Procter & Gamble Co.	18,968.85	3.12%	Q	591.83	
Verizon Communications Inc.	65,785.80	5.05%	Q	3,322.18	
Exxon Mobil Corp.	60,620.00	2.17%	Q	1,315.45	
DFA Emerging Markets Core	45,684.41	1.88%	Q	858.87	
DFA US Core Equity 1	86,848.64	1.51%	Q	1,311.41	
DFA Intl. Core Equity	124,981.43	2.93%	Q	3,661.96	
DFA Intl. Value	16,439.10	3.27%	Q	537.56	
DFA Real Estate Securities	22,477.38	1.76%	Q	395.60	
DFA TA US Core Equity 2	176,272.83	1.46%	Q	2,573.58	
DFA Global 25/75	3,469.25	2.16%	Q	74.94	
DFA Commodity Strategy	5,175.23	0.55%	Q	28.46	
DFA Short-Term Extended Quality	368,022.64	2.18%	M	8,022.89	
DFA Five-Year Global Fixed	24,466.09	2.20%	Q	538.25	
DFA Two-Year Global Fixed	20,398.00	0.94%	Q	191.74	
DFA One-Year Fixed Income	208,569.41	0.59%	M	1,230.56	
DFA National Muni Bond Fund	144,843.10	3.00%	Q	4,345.29	*
DFA Global 25/75	10,407.74	2.16%	Q	224.81	
DFA Inflation-Protected Securities	177,268.15	3.49%	Q	6,186.66	
T. Rowe Price International Bond Fund	109,731.00	2.44%	M	2,677.44	
Bank of America 6.00% 5/28/2020	45,776.25	6.00%	M	2,746.58	
Genl Motors 08/15/2018 7.25%	98,250.00	7.25%	Q	7,123.13	
Genl Motors 11/15/2016 7.375%	99,250.00	7.38%	Q	7,319.69	
Hanks Banks 10.00% Senior Notes	131,986.80	10.00%	M	13,198.68	
JPMorgan 5% CD		5.00%	Q		
Schwab Money Market Fund	66,010.50	0.01%	M	6.60	
	2,228,964.76			70,792.70	

*Est yield due to being a new fund, based on index.

Current Income

Monthly Retirement Paycheck	5,000.00
Gross Monthly Income	5,899.39
Net Surplus / Deficit	899.39

runs on average $1.50 per $100 invested). This increases the return to my clients by keeping costs to a minimum without sacrificing return. I believe the Dimensional Fund Advisors funds represent not only an outstanding value for my clients through low-cost investing, but they also provide access to some of the world's leading economists in modern portfolio design.

You may and should ask questions about any number of specific details when selecting a wealth advisor. I make a point of answering each question as completely and as candidly as possible. Above all, I want my clients to know that they can depend on me for timely, honest answers to any questions they may have about my practice—as well as any questions they may have about their plan, their specific holdings, and how their investments are being handled as we move into the later steps of the overall investment process.

SETTING GOALS TO ACHIEVE FINANCIAL FREEDOM

In our case study, Jake's focus on graduate school, his career, and his desired lifestyle emphasizes perhaps the most important thing about goals: they imply a direction. It's impossible to set a goal that doesn't require taking action to progress toward some clearly defined end. When we set a goal, we are making an agreement with ourselves that we intend to start from where we are and move toward where we desire to be.

Determining the initial direction of that movement—in other words, those initial goals—is the first and most important work I do with my clients. The first question we ask every potential client is: "What are your goals?"

Having a financial advisor ask what your goals are can be daunting. Some people—like me, for example—spend a fair amount of time each day consciously thinking about their goals and assessing their progress. But many other people need prompting and encouragement to generate a clear picture for themselves of where they want to be at some point in the future. That's why in my practice, we break down the initial step in the journey toward financial well-being—goal setting—into several sub-questions that help potential clients think carefully and systematically about where they are now, what their needs are, and how those needs are likely to change in the short, medium, and long term.

Setting Goals: Breaking It Down

1. What are my needs? This question focuses on the present and asks you to spend some time thinking about what it really is that you want your money to do for you.

My father was a skilled carpenter and he used all different sorts of tools, depending on what he was trying to do. If he were cutting the end of a two-by-four, he would use a circular hand saw to make a quick cut. But if he needed to cut a long, very straight piece, he would be more likely to use his table saw since he could use the guide beside the blade to keep the cut true, no matter how long it was.

In the same way, if you want to have your wealth accomplish the purpose you intend, it's important to use the right tool—and there are lots of different financial tools out there. The first step is to have a clear picture of what sort of task you want to accomplish. Do you need a hand saw—or is it time to set up the table saw? Which one do you need?

Like Jake, you may be looking toward funding college expenses and getting started in a career. Or you may be a retired entrepreneur who just sold a company and who now needs to structure your financial holdings to assure a comfortable retirement. You may be a grandparent who wants to make sure that your children and grandchildren inherit a certain portion of the wealth you've accumulated. You may be a young professional trying to determine how much you should spend on buying a home and how much you should keep in reserve against future needs. Or perhaps you are a person who has worked at the same job for years, but you have suddenly come into a large sum of money, through inheritance or some other source, and you have no idea how to deal with this very fortunate, but very intimidating situation. The possibilities are as varied as the people I meet with each day in my financial advising practice. Each situation is unique, and each client comes with his or her own needs and—even more important—his or her own perception of those needs.

As you consider what you need in order to manage your financial assets, you should carefully consider your family situation, any debts or other financial obligations that you have, and your lifestyle desires. Do you have children who are single parents for whom you need to provide support? Are you still making payments on a home mortgage, either for yourself or for a family member? How much of your wealth do you hope to leave as an inheritance—or do you plan to systematically and completely liquidate your holdings in order to provide the lifestyle you desire? To what degree are you willing to limit your present lifestyle so that you can leave something behind for some other person, cause, or organization?

By thinking through these questions, you will begin to see your financial assets as a means to achieve a certain end.

It's important to remember that your needs can change over time, responding to changes in your life circumstances. When answering this question as part of their goal setting, I encourage my clients to consider events and possibilities that might indicate a change in needs and thus the necessity to reevaluate the financial plan down to its basic goals. When your child marries, how will that affect your need to provide partial financial support? What if someone in your family is diagnosed with a chronic medical condition that will require them to receive financial assistance? Will a change in your current employment—positive or negative— have implications for managing your nest egg? Do you anticipate investments that may mature, such as real estate becoming fully paid, interest-bearing notes coming due, or perhaps a high-quality, high-yield bond being called? By identifying certain events at the outset, you can anticipate times when it becomes appropriate to reevaluate what you need from your financial assets, as well as learn how to structure them to provide for changing needs in the most efficient and appropriate way.

2. What are my desires? After considering what you need from your money, it's time to give some thought to your wants, your hopes and dreams. After all, life isn't just about accomplishing the necessities; it's also about achieving personal satisfaction. Once the day-to-day demands of the work world have given way to the more relaxed schedule of retirement, do you want to travel? Do you dream of using your assets to start a foundation for the benefit of some worthy social cause? Do you long to have the financial flexibility to donate your professional skills and services in a developing country for an extended period of time?

One basic problem that many of us have is differentiating between a need and a want or desire. Emotions are powerful; a deep-seated desire for something can cause us to do things that our rational minds caution us to avoid, and yet the desire can be so strong that we behave irrationally—sometimes to our detriment.

It's the same way with your finances. If you're not careful, you can start gratifying desires to the point that you sabotage your long-term needs. That's why your goal setting begins with establishing your needs and distinguishing them from your desires. Once you've met your needs, then you can begin indulging your dreams.

In some cases, paying for your dreams may include a certain amount of judicious reduction in your principal. As long as you have a plan for doing this—a plan that also takes your long-term needs into account—and as long as you stay within the parameters of that plan, some reduction of principal may be acceptable. I've had clients who included this possibility when setting their goals, and I've seen it work well. But it all depends on your particular situation and what you're trying to accomplish.

3. Where do I want to go? In other words, what will you need your financial assets to do for you in the future?

When answering this question, it's useful to think about your goals in the short, medium, and long term—roughly five, fifteen, and thirty years out. Another way to think about this question is to ask yourself: where do you want to be when you're forty-five? Fifty-five? Sixty-five? Older? With advances in medical science, nutrition, and exercise, it will become more and more common-place for people to live longer in retirement than they did during their working lives, which means that setting goals at age ninety will become more and more reasonable and common.

In our case study, Jake's short-term goals focused on paying for and completing graduate school in his chosen field of study. His medium-range goals included purchasing a home and establishing himself in a career, and his long-term goals centered on ensuring that he had the ability to travel and to continue to expand his fund of knowledge and the variety of his experiences, along with build-ing his savings for his eventual retirement.

By contrast, Dorothy, one of my "women in transition" clients (we'll spend more time with her in chapter two), was focused, in the short term, on making decisions about how much of her own money she should spend on buying a home, specifically whether she should use cash or finance some portion of the purchase with a loan. In the medium term, her goal was to ensure that potential future medical expenses would not place an excessive burden on her assets, and in the long term, she had a strong wish to leave some money behind for the benefit of her children and grandchil-dren. Two different clients at two different stages in life had very different answers to this question about where they saw themselves over the short, medium, and long term.

When asking my clients to consider this question, I also ask them to differentiate between their life goals and their financial goals, as well as to think about how these two are interrelated. Toward that end, you should also try to plot your short-, medium-, and long-term goals in both categories.

4. How often should I reconsider, review, or revise my goals? Change is the only constant. No matter how old you are or how far you've advanced in your financial plan, your circumstances can and will change, often in ways that you can't foresee when making the initial plan. This means that from time to time you'll need to reassess your goals to make sure they match with your current situation.

One of the pinnacles of success in any advisory firm is the practice of regular and constant follow-up communication with clients and investors alike. I routinely inquire of prospective clients as to why they are interviewing other advisors, and one of the main reasons they are searching for a new advisor is lack of attention. In fact, statistically speaking, the number-one reason that people are dissatisfied—the reason I hear far more frequently than low investment returns—is a lack of communication and attention to their financial needs. Without regular interactions with your financial advisor, it becomes much more difficult to perform that necessary work of making sure that your financial plan still meets your needs and circumstances. It's simply too important to leave to chance.

That's why the final step of the goal-setting process is establishing the optimal frequency for reviewing the financial plan for possible adjustments. For some, a trimester review is needed; for others, once a year is enough. As long as the client and the financial advisor establish what is appropriate and then stick to that schedule, a client will be able to adjust his or her financial plan as necessary to match major life changes or events.

Of course, in the event of dramatic market movement, whether positive or negative, every client can expect to hear from me and to receive appropriate advice. If an important event occurs that significantly alters a client's circumstances—illness, divorce, birth of a child, sale of a business, whatever—I certainly don't expect them to wait until our next scheduled review to talk with me about their finances. And if a client needs to have a question answered at any time, I'm happy to be in touch. All that should go without saying for any financial advisor worth his or her salt. Establishing periodic reviews of your plan helps you make sure that it continues to match your goals. Any financial plan that does not include a schedule for reviewing the plan itself is incomplete.

To recap: a top reason why people are dissatisfied with their advisor is *not* performance; it's a lack of communication and attention to their financial needs from their advisor.

Case Study: Danny and Sandy (Retirees)

Danny and Sandy had built up a comfortable retirement fund during Danny's forty-year career as an architect. In our goal-setting meeting, I learned that Danny's number-one goal was to avoid outliving his money. That's a pretty common (in fact, universal) goal for my retiree clients.

Danny and Sandy desired a comfortable, upper-middle-class lifestyle. They also had children living in different regions of the country, and they wanted the freedom to travel frequently in order to stay in close contact with them and their grandchildren. They were realistic enough to know that as they got older, travel would be less convenient and desirable, so they intended to enjoy the ability to see their families as much as they could during the next few years, realizing that this would likely be curtailed as they continued to age. They stated that they were willing to dip into the principal of their investment fund to a limited extent if that was what they needed to do in order to support their desired standard of living and their desired level of travel.

Danny and Sandy also had a goal of paying for their grandchildren's higher education. Since their oldest grandchild was in high school, they would need to build some additional liquidity into the portfolio for meeting this secondary—but very important—goal.

As I mentioned before, a challenge many investors face is differentiating between needs and desires. Clients will define these terms differently, and sometimes what one client sees as a secondary objective may be considered primary by his or her spouse or partner. As a wealth advisor, my job is to help clients gain clarity as to how they should define their goals. Thus much of my initial conversation with Danny and Sandy centered on balancing what we determined to be their primary need—having adequate income to support a comfortable retirement lifestyle—with their secondary priority—paying for their grandchildren's higher education and leaving an inheritance for their children and grandchildren.

Danny and Sandy also expressed a fairly high degree of risk averseness. Several times, Danny mentioned to me his worries over the risks that banks and other large financial institutions were taking, risks that were not being disclosed to account holders and investors. Given his concerns about not outliving his money and his substantial expectations for their retirement lifestyle, it became clear to me that a significant part of Danny and Sandy's assets would need to be placed in secure, income-producing investments. Using the answers Danny and Sandy gave to my questions, we were able to clearly define their goals and distinguish their primary needs from their secondary desires, as well as to determine where they saw themselves and what they saw their needs being at different phases of their retirement. Based on all of that, we were able to move forward with a specific financial plan.

Questions I ask in my financial advisory practice emphasize the client's present circumstances—her needs, wants, desires, family situation, and other factors. I then encourage the client to project future aims in the short, medium, and long terms, as well as to consider the points along the way where these goals should be reviewed, adjusted, or even changed altogether. Through their answers, I hope to get my clients to consider not only their present situation or the current market trends and characteristics, but also to take a longer, broader view. I encourage them to consider their wealth and their desires in the context of how those desires will affect the people around them, now and well into the future. Clients can assess how their financial management fits into their family culture, how it affects any causes or organizations that they may be involved with, and what sort of balance they want to strike between saving and spending during retirement years (or for the next ten to fifteen years, depending on the client's age).

Fundamentally, the process allows me, as the wealth advisor, to get a glimpse into my client's family, employment, and investing history. This helps me tailor my advice to the client's experiences, understanding, and overall financial style, which means we have a better chance of communicating accurately and effectively with each other.

OVERCOMING "HOPIUM" AND TAKING ACTION

On October 10, 2008, I and many of my colleagues in the financial world saw the handwriting on the wall. Things were about to get very, very ugly.

In the coming days, I would need to do everything in my power to protect my children's chances to take advantage of the same opportunities that I had enjoyed. If I did nothing to try to change the current state of affairs, I would certainly be letting them down. And what would I say to my clients?

On that day, I had a choice. I could sit back and wallow in despair, waiting to see whether the government or the markets or someone would pull the economy out of the muck, or I could do something about it. It would have been much easier to take the "wait and see" approach, but instead, I was compelled to take action.

To sit back and wait for somebody else to solve your problem requires an attitude I refer to as "hopium"—foolish hope. Hopium allows individuals to ignore new and sometimes unpleasant financial realities, and hopium is what keeps people from making proper plans for the future. It leads to financial ruin.

Hope is indispensable to life. When we lose the ability to hope, we might as well find a six-foot-deep hole and lie down in it. What differentiates true, realistic hope from hopium is that true hope empowers us to take action. When we have hope, we are ready, willing, and able to move in the direction of making that hope a reality. Hope for the future provides motivation in the present.

This book will help you avoid hopium by giving you realistic hope, which is to say the ability to build a solid financial foundation that can withstand the financial storms that may be in store for you. Just as I was compelled to take action to protect my children and clients on October 10, 2008, so too can you take action to shield yourself from future financial catastrophes—as long as you're aware that such catastrophes are possible, and as long as you define your goals carefully in order to take those possibilities into account.

MAKING YOUR GOALS WORK

Dominican University performed a study of a group of people and their goal-setting practices.[3] The study separated participants into five groups and asked each participant to formulate and carefully

---

3. Available online at www.dominican.edu/academics/ahss/undergraduate -programs-1/psych/faculty/fulltime/gailmatthews/researchsummary2.pdf, accessed 28 November 2012.

think about individual goals. Group 1 had no instructions other than the above. Group 2 was asked to take the further step of writing down their goals. Group 3 was asked to write down specific action commitments in addition to their written goals. Group 4 was asked to send their written goals and action commitments to a supportive friend, and Group 5 was asked to do all of the above steps, as well as to make weekly reports about their progress to the supportive friend.

Of course, Group 5 was the most successful at meeting its goals. But what is perhaps even more significant is that participants in Groups 2–5 were slightly more than 50 percent more likely to have achieved their goals than participants in Group 1, who weren't asked to write their goals down. In other words, the simple act of writing down their goals—defining for themselves where they wanted to be—was the single largest factor determining whether or not the study participants were successful.

In my mind, this study illustrates the difference between hope and hopium—hope takes the time to look at the world and set realistic goals for itself. And that's what you need to do to move your financial dreams into the realm of reality.

A friend recently told me a story about his wife, a third-grade teacher. Like many elementary-grade teachers, she has a very organized way of assigning jobs to the kids in the classroom—who gets to lead the class to the lunchroom, who gets to water the plants on the classroom windowsill, who gets to feed the hamster, etc.— in order to teach the students about responsibility and follow-through. Some of the jobs are always more coveted than others, but for different reasons. What could be more desirable for an animal lover, for example, than getting to feed the hamster? Or, for the budding neat freak, the chance to be the cubbyhole monitor and police your classmates' storage habits might be the plum in the pudding.

In addition to the jobs list, my friend's wife had a system of tickets that students could earn for behaving well. For completing assignments on time, working well in a group, remembering to raise hands before speaking, working quietly on a project, providing assistance to the teacher or classmates, and other worthwhile behaviors, students would earn a certain number of tickets. At the end of each week, she would hold an auction for the classroom jobs, and students could bid using the tickets they'd accumulated. Obviously, the students who had accumulated the most tickets could bid more than the kids who hadn't.

But the teacher noticed that one student—we'll call him Matt—wasn't bidding at any of the weekly auctions. She knew he was getting tickets. Matt was a good student who did his work, was helpful to others, was respectful, and so on. Yet Matt watched the auctions from the sidelines and took no action.

The teacher worried about this until the last month of school, when Matt finally revealed his carefully constructed plan. Having hoarded all the tickets he had earned throughout the school year, Matt now owned a monopoly on all of the most desirable classroom jobs. He was the high bidder for everything: hamster care, horticulture, library assistant, lunchroom line leader, the whole nine yards. For that last month of third grade, Matt had a wonderful time doing whatever classroom job he wanted to do that week. He was like Donald Trump and Warren Buffett rolled into one.

I love this story because it typifies the power of goals and what we can accomplish when we have a plan and we act on it. Matt knew where he wanted to be at the end of the school year, and he was willing to be patient and systematic about taking the necessary steps to get there. I don't know how many third-graders like Matt there are in the world, but I'm willing to bet that wherever they are and whatever they choose to do, they are going to end up accomplishing things that their peers can only wish for.

And that is what I hope for you—that you are able to make your goals, dreams, and hopes into realities. You can do it, and in this book I will show you how. But it all starts with having a goal.

STEP 1: DISCOVERING AND SETTING YOUR GOALS

- **What are my needs?** (family obligations, debt commitments, lifestyle requirements)
- **What are my desires?** (difference between a need and a desire)
- **Where do I want to go?** (life goals and relationship to financial goals; short-, mid-, and long-term goals)
- **When is it time to review or revise my goals?**

PLANNING YOUR INVESTMENTS

ONCE YOUR FINANCIAL goals are in place, it's time to make a firm plan for achieving those goals. Your plan is nothing more or less than your road map—your financial GPS—for getting from point A in life to point B without going off your personal fiscal cliff. Without a solid investment plan—and, as I'll continue to stress, the highest level of professional wealth advice you can afford—there's no barrier between you and the risks that are inherent to investing in the financial marketplace. And as the events of October 2008 taught us, those risks can sometimes be great indeed.

A BRIEF HISTORY OF THE END OF
THE WORLD (ALMOST)

I am still convinced that in America, there's more opportunity for more people to make and keep more money than anywhere else on the planet. But that doesn't mean there aren't dangers in the marketplace. The ancient Roman saying, "Caveat emptor" ("let the buyer beware") is nowhere truer than in the financial markets. And these dangers became glaringly apparent in the market meltdown of October 2008.

That crisis was one of the most cataclysmic economic events of our lifetime. Its effects were profound then and they continue to reverberate. For example, whether you agree with the outcome or not, that year's presidential election was tremendously affected by the crash of 2008. Barack Obama promised change, which was what a scared public wanted to hear. The crash also ushered in a severe recession both in the United States and in the rest of the international economic community, one that threatened to tip over into a second worldwide Great Depression.

As with most financial tsunamis, this one started far out at sea, building up over several years before anybody really noticed. It was fostered by many respected financial institutions engaging in practices that were not illegal, but that at best were shortsighted and at worst immoral. In the aftermath, everyone wondered how we ever wound up in a regulatory environment that could permit such excesses.

The real estate bubble that started in 1998 was the harbinger. Like all speculative bubbles, it was bound to burst. Banks were loaning money on inflated real estate prices (with many loans going to borrowers who qualified only through the flimsiest of underwriting tactics), and then repackaging those loans and reselling them. These banks were kicking the can down the road and passing on the risks to the broader credit market for loans that the banks knew would default sooner or later. But as far as the public knew, everything was rosy—real estate prices were climbing, homeowners saw their equity blossoming, banks were lending money hand over fist, and everyone was in a state of bliss.

Still, something wasn't adding up. At the time, I was advising my clients to invest in structured certificates of deposit (CDs) that bore interest rates that seemed much too generous. Banks were eagerly issuing CDs at 9 percent, when by comparison, regular one-year CDs were paying in the area of 2 percent interest. I can promise you that banks don't pay 7 percent over the going interest rate just because they want to be nice to little old ladies. Nevertheless, we took advantage of this unique opportunity and funded CDs to the tune of $1 to $5 million per month.

Why did we do this? Four letters: FDIC! But even though the federal insurance made the investment reasonably secure for my clients, these unheard-of interest rates were the piece that really raised the red flags in my mind.

With the benefit of 20/20 hindsight, we later realized that the banks, who were issuing mortgage loans as fast as they could, needed to bulk up and bolster their reserves at the same rate. They grasped the structured CDs like a lifeline, figuring that an FDIC-insured, high-yield CD would be tremendously appealing to the consumer. And they were right.

These banks, however, were inextricably linked to the fast imploding sub-prime mortgage market and were falling prey to increasingly high loan losses and write-offs. They thought that by bumping up their capital and reserves through the CD offer, they would be able to ride out the coming financial tsunami. But "buying" deposits with above-market CD yields would turn out to be as effective as putting a Band-Aid on a broken leg.

A similar situation developed in Texas in the 1980s, when high-rolling savings and loan associations were using premium-rate CDs to finance aggressive loans on flashy commercial developments. People from all over the country were buying CDs from these S&Ls because of the "Texas Premium." And in the end, when the commercial building boom came to an end, the government ended up taking over lots of Texas S&Ls using a government-designed organization called the Resolution Trust Corporation.

But in 2007 and 2008, the damage wasn't limited to a single region of the country. Huge banks from all parts of the country were bleeding red ink from self-inflicted wounds. Some of the world's major players were going down fast, and nothing and no one could save them from the yawning financial abyss.

America is still the land of hope and opportunity.

As it turned out, things got worse before they started to get better. But they did get better, and though we would see some rough times in the weeks and months following October 10, 2008, the markets would rebound. As I write this, the real estate market shows some signs of life, and some of the backlog of foreclosed properties created when the housing bubble burst in 2007 is beginning to work its way through the pipeline, restoring a more normal relationship of supply to demand. Not that everything is rosy, and it's not that bad things can't happen again. One thing we know about markets is that we must remain vigilant—which is why, again, I recommend working with a financial advisor to stay on top of the overall market situation at any given time. But the disaster was averted—barely—and people are once again making money and building wealth in the financial markets.

HOPE FLOATS

Can you show me anywhere else in the world besides America where independent small investors have such ready access to the mechanics of wealth creation? Where else could you go to gain an entrée to the opportunities that the free markets in this country afford? I can't think of anywhere. Yes, there are risks; after all, risk and reward are directly related. But for those who are willing to take calculated risks, the rewards in the long run can be very sweet.

If I didn't believe in the ability of the markets to survive—if I weren't absolutely convinced that this is still the land of hope and opportunity—I would close my business tomorrow. I have to operate with integrity, and the day when I can't look my clients in the eye and tell them that I know where the opportunities are and that I know how to help them take advantage of those opportunities is the day I shut my doors.

All that being said, hope, dreams, and opportunity don't mean anything if you don't have a plan for turning the goals you've set into a reality. Once you've established your goals—and have taken the extra step of writing them down—it's time to put a plan into place to help you achieve them.

Action Point: Finding the Best Financial Advice You Can Afford

In this book, I have already mentioned the importance of working with a financial advisor or wealth manager; throughout the rest of the book, I'll continue to advocate asking questions of your advisor and expecting prompt, personalized communication in return. But how do you determine what level of service is the highest that you can afford, and how can you exact a higher level of service from the advisor you've got now? The following are a few books or websites (arranged by category) that can help give you some basic knowledge about investing:

I. BEGINNER INVESTOR
Books
- The Investment Answer (Business Plus, 2011)

Websites
- Feed the Pig (www.feedthepig.org)

II. DIY (WITH A LITTLE HELP)
Books
- A Random Walk Down Wall Street: The Time-Tested Strategy for Successful Investing (Tenth edition, W. W. Norton, 2012)
- Winning the Loser's Game: Timeless Strategies for Successful Investing (Fifth edition, McGraw-Hill, 2009)

Websites
- LearnVest (www.learnvest.com)
- 360 Degrees of Financial Literacy (www.360financialliteracy.org)

III. PROFESSIONALLY MANAGED INVESTING
Books
- The Intelligent Investor by Ben Graham (Collins, 2003)
- Global Investing by Roger Ibbotson and Gary Brinson (McGraw-Hill, 1992)
- The Millionaire Next Door by Thomas Stanley and William Danko (Taylor, 2010)

Websites
- KimberlyFoss.com
- Empyrion Wealth Management, my company (www.empyrionwealth.com)
- Financial Planning Association (www.fpanet.org)
- Investment Management Consultants Association (www.imca.org)
- Certified Financial Planner Board of Standards (www.cfp.net)
- Dimensional Fund Advisors (www.dfaus.com)

MY DEFINING MOMENT

My personal plan crystallized just after I had transferred from Sierra College to a four-year university. I had gone to Sierra Community College (at the time, we jokingly referred to it as "BSU," or "Behind Safeway University") and had worked at the drug store full time for a year in order to get some basic courses out of the way and to save money so that I could afford to go to school full time. I remember thinking that Sierra was not much different from high school. Many of the people in my high school graduating class of 400+ who had gone to college were enrolled at Sierra, so even the faces I saw every day were largely the same. All of this contributed to my sense that no matter how well I did at Sierra, I still might not be able to succeed at a four-year college.

Thank goodness for my boyfriend at the time! Mike was a sweetheart, four years my senior, and a manager at the drugstore where I was working. He had graduated from California State University at Chico after he finished high school and knew what getting into a university involved. So along with dating, we talked about college and what it would take for me to be admitted. Mike was incredibly supportive and encouraging during that transitional time in my life and I am forever grateful to him for his belief and support.

After talking through my options with Mike, I decided to take the SAT, which at the time, you could take only once. I did well enough on the test, however, that between my GPA and my SAT score I was accepted at California State University at Chico (CSUC).

Yet even after I had worked so hard to get to college, the experience of being at CSUC was overwhelming. Although I knew I was a hard worker, my self-confidence (like that of many eighteen-year-olds) was still in the developmental stage, and even with my savings and the financial planning I had already done, I wasn't entirely convinced I could even pay for college. In terms of both academics and sheer ability to carry out a long-term plan, university represented a greater level of achievement, one with which I clearly wasn't yet comfortable. Additionally, not one person in my extended family (fifty-two people at the time) had ever attended a four-year university, so there was no guidance or experience my family could offer. I had to do it on my own.

I worked hard at trying to figure out what I wanted my goal of going to college to accomplish. My original intention was to be an architect. I loved thinking about structure and seeing how different elements fit together to make a whole. I enjoyed seeing a process through from the creation of a plan to the final building. I started taking some preparatory courses for architecture in high school, but after a short time, I realized I was no longer as enamored with the study of architecture as I had been. Architects create a building and may participate to some degree in its engineering, but after a while the building crumbles or has to be demolished to make way for a new urban plan. That felt too limiting to me. At about that same time, home computers were really catching on, and I could see that the computer industry was going to change the world. So I decided that I would be a computer science major.

Now that I had some idea of what I wanted to do, I had to figure out how to finance my education. My parents kept me on their health insurance and covered my auto insurance throughout school, but that was all the financial support I got; beyond that, it was up to me. I'd earned enough money by that point—about $15,000 or $20,000—to get me through the first couple of years, and in my junior and senior years I applied for and was awarded two grants. Those plus the income from working in a brokerage office enabled me to pay my expenses: apartment, tuition, books, everything.

I was never sure I fit in at CSUC. To me, it sometimes seemed as if everyone at the school walked around in their pajama bottoms with their backpacks strapped on behind them. I, on the other hand, walked around in a business suit with a briefcase. I was pretty sure most of the other students thought I was a freak. Sure, it was counterculture in college life to wear the flannel suit rather than the flannel pajamas, but I chose to do so because it was simply more efficient. I needed to be dressed professionally, and since I went straight to the office directly after my classes, it made sense to save time and dress for work. I suppose I subconsciously dressed for the job I wanted, not the job I had, as my mother had always coached me growing up. However, I do remember not taking myself too seriously even in college, as I did allow myself to "dress casual" on Fridays (that would be referred to as "casual Fridays" today.)

At that time, I was dating an older man at the university who had a background in finance. He decided he was going to work in the retail side of the industry, and eventually, he got a job with Merrill Lynch. I dated him through the whole process of his application, certification, and training.

The experience of watching him enter the financial industry really made an impression on me. All of the choices he made in his work, down to his portfolio design, showed his sincere belief in the fundamentals of the economy and the importance of free markets. I began to realize, the more I thought about the kind of work he was doing and how fascinating I found it, that the world of finance was where I needed to be.

I had always liked the idea of money and I was becoming interested in computers, which even in the 1980s, I could tell were going to be a major tool in the future of the industry. As I saw it, there wasn't any reason why I couldn't follow a career in the industry. My mother had always said, "You can do anything. Whatever your mind can perceive, your body can achieve, with God's help." I began to turn my fascination with finance into an explicit goal.

My boyfriend went to work for Merrill Lynch while I was a

junior at the university. Not too long after he started there in 1983, I told him about my plan.

"Finance is really fascinating to me, and I think that I might want to become a stockbroker too."

And as I recall, he looked at me and said, "You can't be a stockbroker."

I asked, "Why is that?"

And he said, "Well . . . because you're a girl."

I am sure he didn't mean that statement as it seemed, but our minds sometimes interpret messages differently from how they were intended. In this case, my mind interpreted what he said and responded, "Oh really? Watch me."

That moment changed my life forever. It determined the course I took over the next thirty years, and I'll never forget it for as long as I live. In the years since then, I've thought about what I would say if I could talk to him again. I'd say, "Thank you. You helped me gain absolute clarity about my life's purpose."

Of course, he did it by throwing a challenge in my face. But I've never been one to back away from a challenge. I still had the scars from those blackberry bushes. Suddenly what had been nothing but a dream began to turn into a solid plan, one that I was committed to.

THE NEXT STEP

I decided that Merrill Lynch (or "Mother Merrill," as we affectionately referred to the company then), the biggest and best brokerage firm then, was the company I wanted to work for. So that became my objective. But I was a twenty-two-year-old blond and blue-eyed female, a recent college graduate who had never owned a stock in her life. Why would anyone trust me with his or her life's savings? To compensate for any perceived lack of experience by clients or hiring managers, I needed to get as much real-world experience in personal finance and brokerage as I could.

I began working as an assistant to a local stockbroker, a firm called Birr Wilson. Brian, the broker I assisted, was a wonderful person and boss whose high standard of ethics and client care were obvious to me from day one. I would organize his appointments, make phone calls for him, and help him prepare presentation materials for seminars.

In the next year and a half, I got hands-on experience. I had acquired book knowledge in college, but now I was getting practical experience by helping Brian with trades and writing tickets— all of the grunt work of finance. I learned the language and the daily details concerning stocks and bonds. And gradually, I came to understand the fundamentals of building a successful business as a stockbroker. This experience was invaluable to me in my subsequent career.

Brian would present luncheon seminars that I would coordinate. In the days before email, this work required a lot of phone calls. We would send out a mailer, and then my job was to call the prospects, ask if they had received the mailer, and find out a little bit about them. I'd ask questions: "Have you invested before?" "Do you have a stockbroker that you work with now?" "Have you been successful in your investments?" "How much do you have in the stock market? How have you invested in the bond market?" "Do you own your home outright?" I think Brian intuitively knew that because I was a younger woman, people were more open to giving me information. Without saying so explicitly, he helped me take advantage of this characteristic. When the prospective clients arrived, I would greet them at the door, give them a packet, and seat them so that Brian could present his program. I would get everyone's name and phone number, and then I would follow up and set the appointments for Brian. So I learned a good, basic working knowledge of questions that a planner would ask to help his clients set financial goals.

Brian modeled good client relations. He was charismatic, but he was also sincere. I could tell that he cared about his clients. One of the things he emphasized was the importance of always returning calls. If a client called with a question, he told me that I should try to answer it. But he also said, "Don't BS anybody. Never say anything that you're not sure about," and that if I didn't know the answer to a question, I should tell the client I would have him get back to him or her. He gave me communication skills that I've found to be indispensable to any financial advisory practice.

There were other things I learned while working for Brian that I still make a cornerstone of my practice today. It was here that I began to develop my "drip" philosophy. Brian had a lot of retirees among his clientele who were looking for monthly income. By assisting Brian in his work with these clients, I learned to focus on the dividends and interest that "drip" into a portfolio to provide steady income and gains over time. I also learned from interactions with them that stocks were riskier than bonds, and because these folks were older and had no way to earn a living if they lost their investment, it made sense to put more bonds in the portfolio than stocks. Although I didn't know it at the time, this was the beginning of what I currently use as my asset allocation model.

Brian didn't set out to be my mentor; what I learned from him came from who he was as a person—his character—more than from any explicit lessons he was trying to teach. But I realized that the reason he was successful was because he connected with older folks; he believed that preserving their principal was the most important thing and that one of the fundamental tasks of a financial advisor was to find ways for clients in this category to live off the "drip." Slowly but surely, I was acquiring practical knowledge I needed to flesh out my long-term plan and move toward my goal.

LEARNING THE BASICS

Assisting Brian gave me an amazing education not only in the foundation of good client relationships, but also in building a portfolio for someone. By asking the right questions, listening carefully to the answers, and making recommendations that fit what the client was telling him, Brian proved that he had his clients' best interests at heart. And by utilizing the "drip" philosophy and asset allocation principles, he was able to give his clients something solid that would stand up under a variety of circumstances and market conditions. All of these tools helped me further refine my career plan and develop a solid advisory process that I still follow today.

Just as I needed to learn the basics of building a good advisory practice to achieve my goal, it's important for you as an investor to learn the basics of finance as you devise and implement your goals and plan. You may not think you've got a "financial head," but I don't think it's necessary for every investor to be an expert in the intricacies of stocks, bonds, notes, and derivative investments. It is possible—and necessary—for every investor to grasp some basic principles to maximize his or her chances for success in today's markets.

Think of the next few pages as "Investing 101," where we'll learn a little bit about some of the basics to help your financial plan operate smoothly as it propels you toward your goals.

INVESTMENT BASICS AND EFFICIENT
PORTFOLIO DESIGN

The linchpin of my investment strategy involves using asset allocation and diversification to create what we refer to as "efficient portfolios." This is a term taken from research on modern portfolio theory by Nobel Prize–winning economist Henry Markowitz and others. According to that research, an "efficient" portfolio will generate the maximum anticipated return for the lowest amount of risk. In other words, the most efficient portfolio for a particular expected return rate will be the one that incurs the least risk. In my practice, we use this mathematical principle to design investment portfolios that are robust—that can withstand cyclical market volatility—to help clients achieve their financial goals while still operating within risk parameters that we and the client agree are the most appropriate for the client's situation.

While it is tempting for investors and professionals to focus exclusively on investment returns, Professor Markowitz emphasized the role risk plays in such returns as well. Further, he focused attention on the overall composition of the portfolio rather than following the traditional method of analyzing and evaluating the individual components. He discovered that you could design portfolios based on specific risk-reward descriptions and on the identification and quantification of portfolio objectives.

Markowitz's innovative theory of portfolio design, which has become the new legal standard for prudent investing by fiduciaries, consists of four basic premises:[4]

1. Markets are basically efficient. Markets rapidly process all available information to determine the price of any security. This means that it is statistically improbable to gain a competitive edge by exploiting occasional anomalies. To "beat the market,"

---

4. Also see the following video of Professor Markowitz on portfolio theory: www.youtube.com/watch?v=c5c_Zgn-Bjg.

an investor would have to not only possess the correct insight or information regarding a specific security, but also to be the only investor possessing that information, and he would have to do this consistently over time. With advances in information technology and more sophisticated investors, the markets are likely to become even more efficient.

2. Exposure to risk factors determines investment returns. Academic studies have confirmed that an investor's return is overwhelmingly dependent upon the amount of exposure that an investor has to the specific risks associated with various asset classes. Over time, riskier assets provide higher expected returns as compensation to investors for accepting the greater risk.

3. Diversification reduces portfolio risk and increases expected returns. Including low-correlating asset classes in a portfolio (in other words, asset classes that tend to increase or decrease in value in divergent patterns), even if the assets carry a higher risk when taken individually, can actually reduce overall volatility on a port-folio level and increase expected rates of return. By intentionally designing portfolios that incorporate various degrees of exposure to different asset classes, we can help investors to create the most efficient (highest expected return) portfolio for the level of risk that they are willing to assume.

4. Value-add portfolio management is less costly, and thus increases expected returns. Active portfolio management requires expensive fees and salaries, and these expenses reduce investment returns. The high turnover of securities associated with active management also creates trading costs and higher tax liabilities that are passed along to investors. Active portfolio managers are also susceptible to style drift, which can skew a portfolio's asset allocation to chase recent high-performing specific securities. To avoid these increased costs and liabilities, efficient portfolios will always be managed passively.

Markowitz's theory has been proven by actual portfolio studies, which consistently found that efficiently allocating capital to specific asset classes is far more important than selecting the "right" components within those asset classes. A study by Merrill Lynch showed that in a typical diversified investment portfolio, roughly 90 percent of all the portfolio risk is market risk, and only 5 to 7 percent is specific risk (specific risk being the risk associated with a specific issue, whether this is a stock, bond, or property). The most famous study, conducted in 1986 by Brinson, Hood, and Beebower, determined that on average, 93.7 percent of the variability in the risk and returns of a portfolio could be explained by that portfolio's asset allocation policy.[5]

These and other more recent studies have consistently supported the concept that asset allocation and diversification are primary determinants for portfolio performance, with market timing and security selection playing minor roles. In other words, it's more critical to be in the "right asset class" than to make the "right investment." With these principles in mind, let's take a look at asset allocation, the first and most important aspect of a well-designed investment portfolio.

Asset Allocation

Asset allocation, at its most fundamental level, means nothing more than making sure you have your money distributed appropriately among the major asset classes. Basically, these classes include:

- equities (stocks and their derivative products, which provide the greatest potential for growth in value),
- fixed income (bonds, notes, and other interest-bearing instruments), and

---

5. Gary P. Brinson, L. Randolph Hood, and Gilbert L. Beebower, "Determinants of Portfolio Performance," *Financial Analysts Journal* 42, no. 4 (1986): 39–44.

- cash or cash equivalents (checking accounts, money market accounts, savings accounts, and certificates of deposit).

The premise remains the same today as it was back when Brian was doing it: you put your eggs into lots of different baskets. When a client handed over his assets for investment, Brian might put some of them into a fixed income fund, some into growth-oriented mutual funds, and some into income and growth funds, while retaining enough cash to cover the client's anticipated short-term needs.

The idea is to cover as many bases as you can in the event that a particular market goes south—in which case, your other baskets provide security and protection—or head straight north—in which case, the eggs you're storing in that basket are multiplying at a very pleasing rate.

With very few exceptions, every investor needs both equities and fixed income in his or her portfolio. Especially now that people are living longer and longer in retirement, it's important to maintain a hedge against inflation in your portfolio (a point I'll return to again in more detail later), and this is a task for which stocks are historically well suited. By the same token, however, the stock market's greater volatility means that it's almost always a bad idea to have all your investments there—a bad market or poor performance by one or more of your individual equity holdings would involve risking too much of the value of your holdings. A financial advisor will tell you what mix of equities and fixed income investments are right for you at your stage in life, given your ability to tolerate risk, as well as what mix is best suited to the goals you've set in your financial plan.

Asset allocation: positioning your investments among different asset classes

If, for example, you need a steady income from your investments (as many retired people do), then it will make sense for your asset allocation to be more heavily weighted toward debt obligations and cash equivalents. Corporate bonds, US Treasury bills and notes, tax-free municipal bonds, mutual funds that invest in different corporate and government obligations, government-insured certificates of deposit, money market accounts, and products that guarantee lifetime insurance protection (contingent deferred annuities, or CDAs) for your income stream—all are debt- or cash-based investments that produce the interest "drip" that allows your investments to pay you a regular income.

However, a younger person who is still active in a career is typically more concerned with making sure that his or her investments don't have their value slowly eaten away by inflation. Historically, the number-one hedge against inflation has been the stock market, which trades in shares of ownership of the corporations that produce and sell products and services that drive the world's economy. Some of the world's greatest fortunes have been built in the stock market. Take, for example, Bill Gates, whose innovations at Microsoft drove a huge part of the worldwide dominance of computers and software systems. When Microsoft became a publicly traded company in 1986, Gates's share of company ownership instantly became worth $350 million, and we all know which direction that number has gone in the years since. Likewise, Warren Buffett invested in the failing textile manufacturer Berkshire Hathaway and transformed it into one of the world's largest conglomerates by purchasing stock in companies that he deemed to have value relative to their market price. If you were to have purchased Berkshire Hathaway stock originally at $12 per share, you would own stock worth well over $133,000 per share today.

While it's true that there are immense sums of money to be made in equities, the risks involved are also great. Just ask people who owned Enron stock when the company declared bankruptcy due to illegal accounting practices. That's why it's imperative that your financial plan include an asset allocation mix that's right for you, taking into account your goals and your stage of life. The sad truth is that there is no investment in this world that is completely free of risk. But it's also true that the only way to avoid risk altogether is to do nothing—and doing nothing is by definition not moving you toward your financial goal. This means you must allocate your investments among the different asset classes, knowing that if you establish an intelligent mix that is appropriately balanced among growth, income, and preservation of capital, your losses—while to some degree inevitable—should, over time, be more than compensated for by your gains. It's all about balance and spreading the risk among holdings that have complementary and offsetting risk characteristics. And that brings us to the next important fundamental of efficient portfolio design: diversification.

Diversification Is Your Friend

At first glance, diversification may seem to be pretty much the same thing as asset allocation, since it serves a similar purpose: namely, keeping you from having all of your investments grouped in too few "baskets," which renders them vulnerable to the same risks. But rather than focusing on distributing investments into different asset classes, diversification involves spreading investments among different categories within the same asset type. That means that in addition to allocating your investments among stocks, bonds, and cash equivalents, you should also create diverse holdings for your investments within each asset category.

Identifying investments in many segments of each asset type that are affected differently depending upon the market (assets with "low correlation," in efficient portfolio terminology) is the

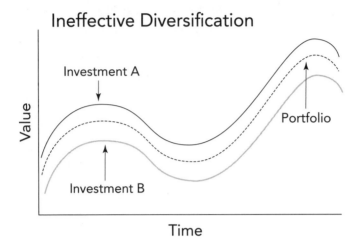

Ineffective Diversification

Value

Investment A

Portfolio

Investment B

Time

Since these two assets are similar in behavior, there is little diversification and therefore, more risk.

key to diversification. The Ineffective Diversification graph illustrates in very simple terms what can happen when an investor owns assets that are inadequately diversified.

Efficient diversification protects you against as many negative bond market scenarios as possible. For example, assume that you invest some of the assets you've allocated to the fixed income category into US government notes, another portion into corporate bonds, another portion into municipal bonds, and so forth. You might also diversify your debt investments by maturity date: some long-term bonds, some medium-term obligations, and some short-term notes. If, with this fixed income portfolio, the corporate bond market takes a negative turn, your holdings in US government debt instruments will become more valuable as bond investors flee the higher risks of corporate debt for the security of government-backed securities. Maturity date diversification protects you against interest rate risk: if interest rates drop, your longer-term, higher-rate bonds will probably increase in value. On the other hand, if interest rates rise, your shorter-term notes will mature sooner, allowing you to recover your principal and reinvest it at higher rates. The illustration below features a hypothetical US government bond index and a hypothetical world government bond index hedged to USD. Adding global issuers to a US bond index substantially reduced overall volatility while the average returns were similar.

For many investors, the S&P 500 represents the first equity asset class in a diversified portfolio. Although the S&P 500 Index is diversified in large US companies, investors can benefit further by adding components. If you only invest in four or five individual stocks, you don't have adequate diversification. Once again, the idea is to position your portfolio broadly enough that a downturn

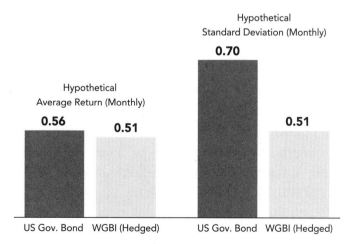

Hypothetical
Standard Deviation (Monthly)

0.70

Hypothetical
Average Return (Monthly)
0.56   **0.51**   **0.51**

US Gov. Bond   WGBI (Hedged)   US Gov. Bond   WGBI (Hedged)

in one industry group—manufacturing stocks, for example—won't have a negative effect on your entire portfolio. The diversified portfolio has provided a higher historical return.[6]

Diversification: positioning your investments among different sectors within a particular asset class

---

Achieving Diversification in Equities

Because the stock market can be especially volatile, diversification within the context of a solid asset allocation strategy is the best protection for the overall value of your portfolio. When new or prospective clients come to me, their equity holdings are all too often a hodgepodge of stocks bought on the basis of various recommendations or opinions, and are insufficiently diversified as to industry group, market capitalization, and investment characteristics.

In such cases, my first step is to help the client formulate a plan to improve the efficiency of his or her portfolio by achieving better diversification in equity investments. This involves repositioning the client's investment to stocks that have low correlation—in other words, whose prices tend to move under different circumstances from one another—thus reducing the overall volatility of the portfolio. The Effective Diversification graph illustrates the effect of owning investments with low correlation.

In my practice, I emphasize three major areas within the equity market: large-capitalization stocks, small-capitalization stocks, and value stocks. These three market factors (or the three-factor model) allow me to help clients achieve optimal diversification of their holdings. Historically, portfolios constructed with

---

6. The text of this paragraph appears in a slightly edited form on the Dimensional Fund Advisors website (www.dfaus.com/philosophy/diversification.html) and appears with permission.

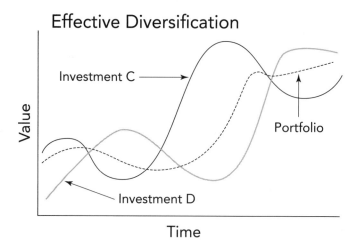

Effective Diversification

Because Investments C and D behave differently, volatility (risk) is smoothed out.

representative holdings from these primary sectors have demonstrated superior rates of return and, in combination, have exhibited lower volatility than any of the sectors experience when considered in isolation.

My "three-factor model" for equity investing:
   1. Large-capitalization stocks—mature companies
   2. Small-capitalization stocks—emerging companies
   3. Value stocks—earnings-distressed companies

The Drip

My concept of the "drip" initially came from the people I observed in my life and practice: lifelong workers who needed their assets to provide a steady income stream for their later years. The majority of asset allocation plans that I've created for my clients have included some portion of investments designed to provide an income flow to the portfolio. Besides the obvious benefits of having a regular "paycheck," the drip also helps mitigate stock market volatility by providing a fixed income. It's important to be aware of the drip, even if you don't need it right now.

Sources for the drip are often provided by investments in the fixed-income or cash-equivalent asset classes: bonds, notes, government securities, and government-insured CDs and money market accounts. These are all investments that earn interest, providing income for the owner. Typically, fixed-income investments are more conservative—and usually safer, in terms of preserving the original invested principal—than equities. Cash, of course, is the ultimate safe haven, but it earns much lower rates of interest than longer-term fixed-income securities.

But you can get drip from other investments too. Many blue-chip stocks have a long history of consistent dividend payments whether it's a good or a bad time for the economy as a whole. Those dividends can be taken in the form of cash, which, when deposited into the investor's account, can add significantly to the drip. Often, conservative investors will purchase stock in utility companies—electric, gas, telephone, and other companies that provide the basic services all of us depend upon—because utility companies typically pay predictable, relatively secure dividends, while still allowing the owner to participate in the value of the underlying stock.

Another way that I help my clients maintain the drip is with the use of a financial instrument called a contingent deferred annuity (CDA). This product can be used in combination with a client's investment portfolio to provide an income stream from the portfolio that is guaranteed for the client's life—a very attractive feature, especially for the growing class of younger retirees. (I'll provide more detailed explanation of CDAs in a later chapter.)

Can You Time the Market?

Short answer: no, at least not consistently over a lifetime.

Market timing—or attempts at market timing—invariably focus on speculation at the expense of wealth accumulation. My clients hire me to help them accumulate wealth, executing a carefully designed plan to help them meet their goals. That means that I don't have time to engage in speculation, nor do I advise my clients to do so.

But we've all heard the stories: somebody plays a hunch and buys a stock one day, then watches it soar in price the next, turning a relatively small investment into a large payoff. Or somebody "has a feeling" and sells a load of stock one day, watching the next day as the market takes a nosedive. The investor looks at the stack of cash in her account, a stack that would've been half its size—or less—if she hadn't sold the stock when she did.

Investment reality rarely matches up with these stories, which I like to call "investment pornography." As a matter of fact, studies have consistently shown that statistically, investment timing represents only about 6 percent of the variance of portfolio values. This means that 94 percent of any portfolio's growth or loss in the marketplace has nothing to do with market timing.

There are several reasons that the money and investment media are so focused on buying "the right stock now" and making a killing on the inevitable market updraft. All those advertisements that promise to tell you about the next penny stock that's poised to become the next Wal-Mart or Apple, as well as all the breathless late-breaking stories in the financial news, are geared around one thing: getting you to create a transaction, to buy something. The advertisers and media don't care and quite frankly don't know whether it's in your best interest, or if it fits your financial goals, or whether the investment is within your risk tolerance range, or anything else. According to the message of market timing, it's all about buying and selling at the "right" time, which is almost always defined as whenever the entity pushing the investment says is the right time. Usually, this is whenever the seller senses the proximity of someone else's hard-earned money.

There used to be a chart that made the rounds in stock brokerage offices. It showed the Dow Jones Industrial average overlaid with some investment scenarios illustrating how someone would have done if they'd invested at a certain point on the Dow and just held the investment for a long-term period, compared with how they'd have done if they'd perfectly "timed the market," buying at every low and selling at every high. The chart clearly showed that if an investor bought and held assets long term, he or she would do almost as well as the theoretical godlike person who would have been able to execute perfect market timing in every bull and bear market for decades. The moral of this story is not hard to figure out.

Naturally, as a wealth advisor, I've seen lots of people who enjoy "playing" the market as if it were some kind of high-stakes poker game. I've even observed individuals who seemed to be addicted to the thrill of taking risks in the market. But that's not how to manage a portfolio for great wealth accumulation, and that's not the behavior I want to see anyone pursue with their "serious" money. I've told clients, "When you decide to retire at sixty-five, do you want the wealth to be there for you, or will you live on the 'thrill' of speculation? Do you want to play in the market today and risk that wealth not being there tomorrow?" Going back to what we discussed in the previous chapter about innate financial behavior, it's true that some people have a basic need to play a stock. For clients like this, I'll set aside maybe 5 percent of the portfolio for them to play with. But I design their portfolio around their serious money, not their gambling chips, and any healthy investment plan you make must do the same.

MAKING YOUR PLAN FIT YOUR GOALS

Once you gain some understanding of investing fundamentals—the market mechanics, the various asset classes, and how asset allocation and diversification fit into your overall strategy—you can move forward with a higher level of confidence. Thanks to the goals you've set, you know what you want to build and you have a simple, working knowledge of the tools you'll be using.

Using this knowledge, you and your financial advisor can structure a plan that will help you gain the maximum benefit from your investments and enable them to move you toward the goals you established early in this process. Metaphorically speaking, the fundamentals are basic materials—the mortar and steel—of the structure that you're assembling—your financial objectives and goals. Now that you have these building materials at your disposal, it's time to start assembling them, giving shape and reality to your dreams and goals. It's time to design the specifics of your plan.

Case Study: Scott and Mary ('Tweeners)

Scott was a successful engineer who made some astute investments earlier in his career that put him in a very favorable position as he and his wife Mary began to look toward his early retirement. Furthermore, as an engineer, Scott had an intuitive understanding of the benefits of the asset allocation and diversification model we developed; the concepts behind efficient portfolio design appealed to his quantitative orientation, and he grasped them quickly.

Being 'tweeners—nearing retirement age but still working and generating a substantial income—Scott and Mary needed the safety of principal, but also had to protect their long-term goals (a comfortable retirement) against the encroachment of inflation. At their relatively young age, the long-term effects of inflation had to be taken into account in order to make sure their assets could fund several decades of retirement for both of them.

As I developed the plan for Scott and Mary, it became clear to me that while their goals, dreams, and objectives indicated that we should pursue investment strategies that would provide

Example of a 40/60 portfolio allocation			
4.4%	DCMSX	DIMENSIONAL FUND ADVISORS Commodity Strategy	$46,805.13
7.1%	DFEOX	DIMENSIONAL FUND ADVISORS US Core Equity	$74,695.55
15.0%	DFEQX	DIMENSIONAL FUND ADVISORS Short Term Extended	$159,289.83
10.4%	DFGBX	DIMENSIONAL FUND ADVISORS 5 Year Global Fixed Income	$110,184.87
5.5%	DFIHX	DIMENSIONAL FUND ADVISORS 1YR Fixed Income	$57,943.80
3.8%	DFREX	DIMENSIONAL FUND ADVISORS Real Estate Security	$39,822.80
14.6%	DFTCX	DIMENSIONAL FUND ADVISORS TA US Core Eqty	$154,624.39
10.9%	DFTWX	DIMENSIONAL FUND ADVISORS TA World Ex US	$115,984.12
10.0%	DIPSX	DIMENSIONAL FUND ADVISORS Inflation Protected Securitie	$105,466.40
4.9%	RPIBX	T. Rowe Price Intl Bond	$51,519.07
4.6%	VFIIX	Vanguard GNMA Fund	$49,172.61
91.1%			$965,508.57
8.9%		Money Market	$93,887.91
100%		Total	$1,059,396.48

for security of principal, we also needed some long-term growth characteristics to outpace the rate of inflation. During my discovery meeting with them, I determined that they had a high enough tolerance for risk to allow them to participate in the stock market as long as we followed our diversification guidelines.

Accordingly, we committed 40 percent of their funds in an equity portfolio containing large-capitalization, small-capitalization, and value stocks, both in the US and in selected foreign markets. Then, we positioned 60 percent of their investment assets—at that time, held primarily in cash and cash equivalents—into a fixed-income mix that was positioned at the optimal point on the yield curve to provide maximum income with minimum volatility. Based upon their goals, their financial situation, and the understanding they had of the fundamentals of investing, we were able to work together to develop a plan that would accept a reasonable risk in order to bring in the best possible rate of return.

Case Study: Dorothy (Women in Transition)

Dorothy's was an entirely different story. She was well into her retirement years when she came to see me, and one of the first things I learned about her was that as a result of growing up during the Great Depression, she was scared to death of the stock market. (This is not unusual among investors of her generation.) As a woman in her later years, Dorothy had less reason to worry about inflation than Scott and Mary, so we determined that safety of principal would be our main focus.

Yet Dorothy also needed to establish a dependable income "drip" from the generous inheritance she had received from her deceased husband. At the time of our discovery meeting, federally insured CDs were paying less than 5 percent interest, even at very long maturities. We had a dilemma: how could we generate

Dorothy's Allocation

Current: 100% Fixed

Proposed: 100% Fixed

Current Equities:

%:	Security Name:	Ticker:		Current Value:	Buy/Sell:		Proposed Value:	%:
0.0%	N/A	N/A						0.0%
0.0%								**0.0%**

Current Fixed Income:

%:	Security Name:	Ticker:		Current Value:	Buy/Sell:		Proposed Value:	%:
13.7%	DFA Inflation-Protected Securities	DIPSX	$	70,368.84		$	70,368.84	13.7%
16.6%	DFA One-Year Fixed Income	DFIHX	$	84,836.84		$	84,836.84	16.6%
14.1%	DFA Two-Year Global Fixed	DFGFX	$	72,124.89		$	72,124.89	14.1%
16.9%	DFA Short-Term Extended Quality	DFEQX	$	86,697.56		$	86,697.56	16.9%
10.4%	T. Rowe Price International Bond Fund	RPIBX	$	53,108.01		$	53,108.01	10.4%
7.8%	Vanguard GNMA Fund	VFIIX	$	39,804.90		$	39,804.90	7.8%
0.0%	JPMorgan CD 5%	N/A	$			$	74,100.34	14.5%
20.6%	Schwab Money Market Fund	MMF	$	105,322.81		$	31,222.47	6.1%
100.0%			$	**512,263.85**		$	**512,263.85**	**100.0%**

| **100.0%** | | | $ | **512,263.85** | | | | **100.0%** |

a better income from Dorothy's assets without incurring an unacceptable level of risk?

Because of my relationships in the banking industry, I was able to structure a certificate of deposit for her with a fifteen-year maturity—much longer than those generally available to the public—and a correspondingly high interest rate. But the CDs we structured for Dorothy were callable after one year, which meant that the issuing bank could, at its option, redeem the CD as early as one year after the issuing date.

In other words, we dealt with Dorothy's aversion to market risk by utilizing investments that offered government insurance and a better rate of interest than would have been otherwise available to her. She was exposed to credit risk with regard to the underlying bank, but since her principal was insured, she was willing to tolerate the plan. This was all consistent with her overall life situation, as her age made her less apt to be impacted by the long-term effects of inflation.

Again, as with Scott and Mary, we took into consideration Dorothy's background, life situation, risk tolerance level, and goals in designing an investment plan for her that balanced her need for income with the level of risk she was willing to tolerate. A good financial plan developed between you and your wealth advisor should take into account the same factors to provide results that match your individual situation and goals.

A PLAN THAT LETS YOU SLEEP AT NIGHT

Because of her background, Dorothy was highly averse to the risks inherent in the stock market. This made it imperative that we take her risk-averse nature into account as we structured her asset allocation plan. And that's an important final factor to consider: will your investment strategy allow you to sleep at night? Because if it won't, then either you need to have a better understanding of how the risks you're taking are helping you meet the goals you've set, or you need a different strategy that involves less risk.

Now, remember what I said earlier: there is no investment that is free of risk. None. Even government-insured CDs carry risk beyond the basic risk that the government may default and not be able to pay off its depositors. CDs and all fixed investments carry interest-rate risk: if you lock your money in a bond for one, five, ten, fifteen years, or more and interest rates rise, you'll be stuck with a lower-yielding investment until it matures, or you'll risk selling your bond for a loss in the principal. Fixed investments also carry inflation risk. When you keep money in cash or cash-equivalents, CDs, or bonds, there is a very real risk that the constant creep of inflation will erode your money's value. For people who have a very long-range goal for their investments, inflation risk absolutely must be taken into account.

Example of decrease in the value of a five-year bond with a 5-percent coupon:
- *1 percent rise in interest rates: decrease of 4.49 percent*
- *2 percent rise in interest rates: decrease of 8.97 percent*
- *3 percent rise in interest rates: decrease of 13.46 percent*

But most people who are very risk-averse tend to think of only one type of risk: market risk. Like Dorothy, they think about cataclysmic market crashes like the one in 1929 or the more recent ones in 1987, 2001, and 2008, and they can't imagine taking that type of risk with their money. Market risk—the risk that your investment will be reduced by unfavorable market forces—is certainly something to be concerned about. But as I said above, it isn't the only type of risk.

The other factor that is very important in evaluating your risk tolerance is your time horizon. Are you planning to retire very soon, and do you need liquidity from your funds to maintain your lifestyle? Is that money intended to pay for college for a grandchild who is about to graduate from high school? Are you planning to use some or all of your investments within the next five years to finance the purchase of a home or to make a down payment on a business opportunity? The shorter your time horizon, the more liquidity you need and the less market risk you want to assume in your portfolio. The longer your time horizon, generally speaking, the less you should be concerned by temporary market fluctuation and the more you should be concerned about the near certainty of inflation and what it will do to the purchasing power of your assets.

When building an investment plan, it's very important to consider the kinds of risks you are and are not willing to assume. Once you've done that—and once you're sure that you've matched your plan with your goals and with the time you have for achieving them—you can sleep at night, knowing that you've assembled a vehicle that will travel the route you've laid out.

When you've reached this point—you have written an investment plan (your goals) and created your investment plan, bearing in mind the fundamentals of efficient portfolio design—it's time to make the commitment and begin the journey.

STEP 1: DISCOVERING AND SETTING YOUR GOALS

- **What are my needs?** (family obligations, debt commitments, lifestyle requirements)
- **What are my desires?** (difference between a need and a desire)
- **Where do I want to go?** (life goals and relationship to financial goals; short-, mid-, and long-term goals)
- **When is it time to review or revise my goals?**

STEP 2: PLANNING YOUR INVESTMENTS

- Do I know the fundamentals of investing?
- What does my asset allocation currently look like?
- What does diversification mean?
- Why shouldn't I try to time the market?
- What types of risk can I tolerate?

COMMITTING TO YOUR PLAN

THE ONLY PROBLEM with a plan is that it must be executed to achieve its purpose. I realize this statement sounds like the most common of common sense, but you'd be surprised how many people I've seen formulate great goals, create ambitious plans . . . and stop right there. Those people don't achieve their goals because they never take the all-important step of commitment.

I love this quote from Art Turock, the business consultant and motivational speaker: "There's a difference between interest and commitment. When you're interested in doing something, you do it only when circumstances permit. When you're committed to something, you accept no excuses, only results." I appreciate the way he draws a distinction between being interested and being committed. Interest is fine as a starting point, but if you're ever going to accomplish anything—in your finances, in your personal life, in improving your health, in learning something new—you've got to become committed to your purpose.

Another great illustration of the difference between interest and commitment: do you know the difference between the attitudes of the chicken and the pig toward achieving the goal of a bacon-and-eggs breakfast? The chicken is interested; the pig is committed.

TAKING THE PLUNGE: MERRILL LYNCH

By the time I'd graduated with my business degree from California State University at Chico, I had acquired a great deal of hands-on experience as Brian's assistant. I knew the terminology, I knew the products, and I knew how clients thought and what made them tick.

But it wasn't until I landed the position at Merrill Lynch that I actually felt I had made it in the big leagues. I was determined to settle for nothing less than a career with the world's largest brokerage firm—to be on the same playing field with the most experienced brokers anywhere. It was Mother Merrill or bust!

The prospect was daunting. One of my mentors in the finance world had already warned me about the "no girls allowed" sign hanging above the entrance to the "serious" brokerage firms, and I was fresh out of college, a wide-eyed young adult from a small town. Even with solid experience under my belt, I wondered how I could possibly gain the confidence to go in and refute the reasons someone might throw at me as to why I wouldn't be able to make it in the big leagues. How could I convince them to trust me with any kind of funds? What chance did I have at building a financial advising practice?

BE PREPARED, NOT SCARED

To better my chances, I interviewed with other firms, basically treating each interview as a dress rehearsal. When I applied to Merrill Lynch, the skills I had developed in those practice interviews were enough to get me past the first interview I was prepared.

In the next phase of the interview process, the hiring managers put those of us who'd passed the first interview into a brokerage simulation. We went into a big room with cubicles and telephones, and each of us had a list of contacts and phone numbers in front of us. The simulation was intended to recreate an actual session of calling clients, making recommendations, fielding questions and complaints, and doing as many as possible of the other activities that fill a typical day at a busy stock brokerage firm. Luckily for me, the daughter of the manager at Birr Wilson was also interviewing and had already gone through the Merrill Lynch simulation. She gave me some idea of what I could expect, which was a break for me.

There were thirty candidates in the room. The hiring managers sat each of us down in a cubicle with a phone and gave us scenarios for each contact. The "clients" were being played by Merrill Lynch brokers. For example, I would call "Brad."

"Hi, this is Kimberly Foss from Merrill Lynch. How are you today?" I would then proceed to convince "Brad" that a certain stock would be the right financial choice for his situation.

The investments we were to offer in these scenarios came from a specific list of different stocks and treasury bonds. On the list were two high-flying stocks—very aggressive, high-risk/high-return investments. These high-flying stocks had a huge commission because the company wanted to push the stock. Therefore, selling the high-fliers would, in an actual trading situation, give the broker a higher incentive payout. Additionally, the data we were given offered us theoretical big-screen TVs, trips, and other incentives for selling the high-risk/high-return stocks. The hiring managers wanted to see if we would do the right thing for the client rather than for ourselves.

We read our scenarios, then dialed the first number on the list. The people on the other end of the phone knew what they were doing, and they knew what I was trying to do. These people were brokers who over the course of their careers had heard it all, and they made sure I and my fellow simulation callers heard plenty too.

Many of the scenarios involved people who were retiring and who were looking for secure income or conservative investments. In one, a woman named "Mrs. Smith" had a great deal of money—something like three million dollars that she'd inherited. She was seventy-three years old, was recently widowed, and had trusts. According to the scenario, anytime her broker would call to sell her anything, she would accept.

I was explaining various investment options to "Mrs. Smith," and she was extremely enthusiastic about the high-risk stocks, almost trying to buy them before I could finish my explanation. All I had to do was say the word, and she would buy a boatload of the high-commission "stock of the month."

I said, "Well, yes, I do have that kind of a stock for you. I do have that available. But honestly, Mrs. Smith, you are seventy-three years old. You really need a steady income . . . you don't need to put your principal at risk. As they say, the client is always right, but if you are looking for honest guidance from me, your advisor, I wouldn't put my mother into that stock. And I wouldn't advise that to you, either."

At the end of the simulation, we received our grades: A, B, C, D, F. A prospective hire had to get a B or better to move on to the next level. Two of us made it: myself and another gentleman who was changing careers at thirty-two years old.

I staggered out of the simulation room, mentally and physically exhausted. But I had cleared another hurdle on the path to my goal. So I went back for the next round of interviews, and the next, and the next.

Being hired at Merrill Lynch was a very competitive process, and it stretched me to my limits. I had one pair of pumps that matched my suit, and I would shine those shoes and always wear nylons (and still do, as in my opinion, it is the proper attire in the business world). Knowing that I was a blonde and that people had preconceptions about blondes, I tried to put my hair up in a way that looked professional. I wore the same suit to each interview (after all, I was still on a recent-graduate budget), but since I was always interviewed by a different person, nobody ever noticed.

After about four interviews, I made it to the final round. It was like getting into the World Series. I had just graduated from college in June, and if I got the job with Merrill Lynch, I would start in July, giving me only a couple of weeks of vacation—unless, of course, I didn't make it. The Merrill Lynch offices were on the twenty-second floor of a high-rise office building in downtown San Francisco. The interview process was the first time I'd ever been in San Francisco by myself, and I feared I might miss a bus or otherwise throw off the whole thing.

On the day of the final interview, I entered an enormous office with a huge window and intimidating plush furnishings. By then I was thinking, *This is it. This is the eleventh hour. I can't waver now. I must commit.*

The manager, Richard Smith, introduced himself, and I shook his hand. Then he immediately began to ask questions, looking at me and then down at his notes. I answered every single one as quickly as I could; boom, boom, boom, boom.

After he had asked me most of the standard questions, he looked down at his notes again, seeming to be lost in thought.

I said, "You know, Richard," (I was definitely taking liberties here by calling him by his first name, but I felt I needed to level the playing field to gain traction). "If I may interrupt a minute. You've asked me so many questions, and I've answered every single one of them, but I still see that you're in a quandary, if I may say so, about whether or not you should hire me."

"Yes," he said.

"May I speculate on why that is?"

"Sure," he offered.

I began without hesitation. "I think you're concerned about my age. I know you can't say that here, but I sense your concern regardless. Let me assure you I have what it takes to be a stockbroker. And if you're concerned with how clients will think of working with a relatively young woman, I can dress up and put on a long skirt and heels, put my hair in a bun, put all my makeup on, and carry the briefcase with confidence, no doubt. But it really comes down to how hard you work. And after a couple of years in this business, if I've survived this, you won't have to worry about what clients will think about my age. This face will have plenty of wrinkles on it, and my age won't matter anymore."

He broke up laughing.

"Did I answer all your questions?" I asked.

"Yes, you did," he replied.

I shook his hand and walked out. Two days later, I got the job.

I felt absolutely fabulous—vindicated even—until just after I started working at Merrill, when I was told—by my regional manager, no less—that the only reason I'd gotten the job was because they had to fill a quota. "Honestly," he said, "we don't expect you to be here in three months."

I calmly responded, "Really? Watch me."

OUT OF THE FRYING PAN, INTO THE FIRE

For the first three months at Merrill Lynch, we trained and became familiar with basic procedures. Then it was time to take the Series 7 Securities Licensing Examination. My manager told me that the company would pay for the test, but that I would only have one chance to pass. "This is it. We're not paying you to try, try again. Study and use your time wisely." This was when I became best friends with my Franklin planner, which I still use today and require my employees to use when managing their time. I think that a disciplined approach to time management is essential for anyone who wants to be successful in this business. There is a connection between writing down your goals on a daily basis and marking them off that doesn't exist with electronic time management methods.

Unfortunately, although I used my time wisely, I didn't pass the exam. I studied so hard, but the exam was mostly about stock options, and that was one area I wasn't interested in at the time. I received a sixty-nine, one point shy of a passing grade of seventy. I had flunked the exam, and now my job at Merrill Lynch was in serious jeopardy.

I was devastated. Everything I had worked for up to that point was directed toward having this job at Merrill Lynch; it was my whole world! I pleaded my case with my manager. He said that he would allow me to take it one more time, but that I would have to take it within the next month, and this time they wouldn't pay for the exam fee. I was grateful for the second chance and vowed not to fail again.

I was committed to staying with Merrill Lynch, and I worked out a plan to make sure that this time, I would pass the Series 7. I decided that I would take a "cram course" to better my chances, one that cost $600—money that I didn't have. This was the only time in my life when I had to borrow money from my parents. It was a humbling experience, one that was made even harder because I knew my parents didn't have much money to lend. But I told them that I would pay them back immediately, and they fronted me the money.

I took the course, took the exam, and this time, I passed! Within my first month after passing and starting work in earnest, remembering what my parents had always told me—"you pay your debt back first, and then you play"—I returned the $600 they had loaned me. Then I started to build my business.

In 1984, brokers started out by receiving a monthly "draw" of around $3,000—the nipple, as I often referred to it. While on the draw, I started at zero every month. I had to do as many trades or sales as were needed to cover the draw, and then if I got beyond that, I could start to make a lot of money. For example, suppose I sold someone $10,000 worth of a mutual fund that had a 4 percent payout to the broker (what we called "production credit"). Four percent of $10,000 is $400, which meant I had to sell $75,000 of that investment per month to meet my draw. In other words, I had to have at least seven and a half clients who were willing to invest $10,000 in that investment just to break even and pay the "draw" back to Merrill Lynch. If I earned enough production credit to get beyond the draw, the house got two-thirds of the money and I got one-third. That was a pretty high bar for someone to clear at twenty-two years old, starting out from zero.

How does a novice broker with no family connections and no "old money" relatives or friends get clients? By cold-calling: that hated ritual so well known and so universally despised by stock-brokers everywhere. Smiling and dialing.

I loathed it. The rule of thumb was that out of 100 calls, I would get ten people interested, of whom one would become a client. Since I was on the West Coast, I'd sell stocks and bonds and make all my trades from six in the morning until one in the afternoon, when the New York markets closed. I would take a break, and then I would go back and cold-call. Then I would take a break for din-ner before cold-calling from 7:00 to 9:00 p.m.

Every month I carried the monkey on my back: making hun-dreds of cold calls, talking to as many people as I could convince to listen to me, scratching hard for every trade and every mutual fund sales ticket, sweating it out as I tried to cobble together enough production credits to validate my draw from the company so that they wouldn't kick me out onto the street. I'd struggle all month, and then the next month would come around, the counter would roll over to zero, and that same monkey would just be sitting there, waiting for me. And again, off I went.

To this day, I have nightmares about that time in my life. In the dream my manager calls me in and says, "Okay, it's almost the first of the month. You've only made two trades. What are you going to do?" I panic, and then I wake up in a cold sweat, thinking, *Oh, thank God! I don't have to do that anymore!*

I bought into the whole Merrill Lynch corporate persona. I truly wanted to please my managers and to do well for myself and the firm. I was the girl, so I was different. There were only three women among the twenty-eight brokers in the office, and of those twenty-eight brokers, about twenty-five of us were younger than thirty. We were young, but the office wasn't totally free of a few premature gray hairs.

The normal path to building a business was to accumulate enough cash under management to go off the draw altogether, so that all the production credit we earned would go to us and to the company in the one-third/two-thirds split. We had been coached to go off of the draw as quickly as we possibly could. It was embarrassing to me, a go-getter, to stay on the draw. I wanted to please my manager and I especially wanted to prove everybody wrong who said that I'd been hired because of a quota; I wanted to prove that I was actually smart and worked hard and could do this. So I went off the draw very early, within six or eight months of starting at Merrill.

As a result, I didn't make a lot of money at first, and instead spent my time trying to build my client base—my "book." The carrot dangling from the end of the stick was the prospect of doing well enough and earning enough money to get off the floor in the bullpen and get a private office on the side of the building. That became my new big goal, and within a year and a half, I got one of the coveted private offices. I'd built my book, and was "in" at Mother Merrill!

MY COMMITMENT GOES TO THE NEXT LEVEL

Through hard work and commitment, I had achieved my initial goals. But over time, it became apparent to me that in order to really meet my clients' needs and conduct my business in the way that made sense to me, I would have to step my commitment up one more notch: I would have to start my own firm.

As I'd learned working with Brian, I gathered information about the clients in my book to help me make the best financial decisions for them. Merrill didn't seem too happy about that. At the time, the dominant sales culture was what I thought of as the "product-of-the-month club." The manager would come around to all of the brokers and tell us that the company had bought some number of dollars' worth of an IPO (an "initial public offering" of a stock or investment package). The manager would then assign each of us a certain number of shares to sell. We were expected to call everyone in our books and place those IPOs, whether that was the best thing for the clients or not.

Over time, it became clear to me that my true commitment was not only to my personal goals and to the financial industry but also to my clients' welfare. I wanted to do the right thing for them every single day, regardless of how many shares of a given IPO the company wanted me to sell. And even though I eventually became the number-two producer in my office at Merrill Lynch, I came to realize that if I wanted to do what I knew in my heart was right, there was no avoiding the next step: going out on my own. And so, in mid-1989, I took the plunge. I rented office space and I started

Erickson & Associates, my own little Registered Investment Advisor business.

One of the most important initial decisions I made toward honoring my commitment to my clients was to operate on a fee-based model rather than on a commission-based model as was done in the brokerage industry. The evolution toward fee-based financial advising was in its infancy, but I was convinced, all the way back in 1989, that this was the way I had to do business.

In a commission-based firm, a broker receives production credit whenever the client makes a transaction, buying shares of an IPO, buying a bond, etc. In a fee-based firm, advisors' compensation is directly proportional to the overall performance of the assets under management (AUM). In other words, if I am managing a million-dollar portfolio, my fee is based on a percentage of the amount of the overall portfolio. If the assets in the portfolio grow, the fees grow as well, but if the assets depreciate, so do the fees. There are no conflicts of interest in doing what is right for my clients each and every day. And the only way I make more money is to make sure that my clients' assets grow first.

As I said, not many people were doing business this way at the time, and I caught a lot of flak from other brokers. Few wanted to step outside the bounds of the established transaction-driven culture, and I suppose that having a fee-based firm setting up shop nearby perhaps made them feel a bit nervous and exposed. Nevertheless, I believed even then that the industry as a whole was shifting toward a fee-based model. If I was going to help my clients build wealth, I had to take risk too. If I was going to ask clients to trust me with their hard-earned money to help them secure their retirement and meet their other financial goals, it was only right to be on the same side of the table. Basing my fee on how successful I was as a steward of their assets seemed to be the only option.

*In **fee-based financial advising**, the client's fee to the advisor is based upon a percentage of assets under management rather than on commissions for transactions.*

Clients began to rally around my concept and business model, and my firm grew through word-of-mouth to clients' friends, associates, and family members. My goal when I opened my doors had been to break even, including all startup costs, after two years. Instead, I broke even after the first year.

IMPORTANCE OF COMMITMENT

Only commitment to my goals and my plan saw me through the obstacles I faced on my path to finding my true career niche. The road to investment success can be just as challenging. The market might take a tumble, interest rates might go against you, tax laws might change. Any number of things might happen—many that can't be foreseen—that could make you question the plan you've put in place. But commitment to your course is the only way past these obstacles to your goals. You can't allow temporary discouragements or difficulties to deter you from continuing on the path that you've charted.

To be sure, there will be some bumps along the way. But if your financial advisor has carefully listened to your needs and goals and has designed your investment plan to take the possibility of these difficulties into account, and if you have committed to your plan and to your financial advisor, you can face these temporary dislocations with confidence. The commitment phase is where you can most clearly see the advantage of working with a financial professional versus doing your own trades. If you cannot afford an ongoing dialogue with a professional, consider scheduling a single consult with one when you've built your plan and before you commit to it.

Commitment to a specific plan is so central to my investment philosophy that the entire third step of my clients' program is built around it. Once we've established a client's goals and once we've developed a plan designed to help the client meet those goals, we schedule a commitment meeting to implement the plan we've developed. At the commitment meeting, we do the following:

- Make decisions on direction
- Verify our mutual agreement to proceed
- Draft all necessary documents
- Put investments in motion

Commitment is a two-way street, and just as I require that clients commit to the financial plan we've devised, I require my firm to make a similar commitment to our clients. The following are some of the pledges we make to clients at the commitment meeting:

- In addition to the expertise of our in-house strategic team, we connect clients to our network of professionals in other areas that are important to their finances, including the legal and accounting fields.
- The client always retains the ultimate decision-making authority over how his or her assets are invested, no matter what guidance our advisors offer.
- We respond to questions regarding a client's financial situation within twenty-four hours at most, and in most cases within twelve hours.
- Above all, we exercise the highest professional ethics when building and managing our clients' portfolios.

Action Point: Choosing the Right Financial Advisor

In deciding who will help you manage your financial assets, the first and perhaps best criterion you can use is, "Will this person communicate effectively with me?" I have mentioned that the number-one reason people end a relationship with a financial advisor is due to ineffective or nonexistent communication. Clients have told me that with their previous financial advisor, they were relegated to two appointments per year, and if they used those appointments, they were done. One client had spent ten years with such a broker, which represents an amazing amount of patience, in my view, for a client to show toward a firm that seems to have no time to communicate with the people whose money they're managing.

In many ways, the brokerage relationship is like the one between a patient and a doctor. To be the best steward of your own health, not to mention the smartest consumer of health care services, you should have certain questions on the tip of your tongue as soon as your fifteen-minute consult clock begins ticking. What is this test for? When will I get the results? How many times have you done this procedure? Why do I need this treatment? What are the alternatives? And so on. In a like manner, you should be able to ask your own advisor any question you want about your portfolio. If you have a limited number of meetings with your advisor each year and you cannot afford to move up to the next level of service, get the best advice your dollar can buy by coming to meetings with a list of questions prepared, or email them ahead of time if possible. I truly believe that the biggest mistake most clients make with their advisor is the failure to ask questions.

If I know that a prospective client has come to me after working with another financial advisor or stockbroker, I use part of the discovery meeting to ask what caused them to leave their previous advisor or stockbroker. The precipitating event could be a call that didn't get returned, a question that went unanswered, or some other straw that broke the camel's back. What prompts clients to leave an advisor is less often a major breach of trust and much more often the cumulative effect of feeling ignored or brushed aside over a long period of time. I intentionally try listen first and be heard last, as this results in my clients intuitively feeling that they have been heard and that they can communicate freely at any time—with or without an appointment.

As we've discussed earlier in the chapter, there are two primary classes of financial advising: transactional and consultative.

- Transactional brokers or advisors are primarily focused on recommending a variety of investment products to their clients. They tend to be commission-based advisors, compensated on the basis of the transactions they perform.

- Consultative advisors, in contrast, take a more holistic approach to investing. Their job is to figure out, in consultation with you, your financial strengths, weaknesses, needs, and goals. Consultative advisors are generally compensated on a fee basis, based on the number of assets they manage for the client.

I strongly believe that the fee-based system is in the client's best interest, and for these and other reasons, I recommend working with a financial advisor who adopts a consultative approach.

Case Study: Dorothy

When Dorothy, whom we met in chapter two, arrived at the mutual commitment meeting, she remained adamant that she wanted nothing to do with the stock market. As noted earlier, we were very careful to recommend investments for her that were geared toward preservation of capital and a secure income stream, primarily focusing on structured certificates of deposit (CDs) with a higher interest rate than that available to retail bank customers. Thus, we were able to provide a more generous income stream for Dorothy while still providing government-backed protection for her invested principal.

Now that we had a plan in place that matched up with her goals and her risk tolerance, it was time for Dorothy to commit. The strategy we had designed called for us to move her assets from the money market accounts where they were being held (accounts which, because they are cash-equivalents, pay very little interest) into the longer-term structured CDs and insured high-grade tax-exempt bonds. For Dorothy, this represented a venture into uncharted financial territory—she had lived through the Great Depression as a child, and she remembered all too well what happened to people's money when the stock market dropped and the banks went under.

At the commitment meeting, I always go over what clients can expect from me and my firm. I assure them once again that we have assembled our investment recommendations based on the goals they have shared with us, and I go over the reasoning and the rationale for how we intend to proceed with setting up the strategy and managing the investments. As we discussed this, Dorothy asked a number of questions about the security of her principal, the nature of the US government's FDIC insurance, how bond insurance works, the timing of the interest payments, and several other aspects of investing. I was aware of the uncertainty she felt toward the stock market, and so my firm made sure to show our commitment to her by explaining everything about the investment plan until she was comfortable with placing her assets under our management according to the strategy we had worked out together.

Once everything was explained to her satisfaction, Dorothy signed the paperwork and we initiated her investment plan.

COMMITMENT BASICS

There are three fundamental questions that we ask every client to answer before coming to the commitment meeting:

1. How do I enact my plan?
2. How do I commit to that plan?
3. What problems will challenge my commitment?

Enacting your plan. For some investors, enacting their plan may not be as simple as writing a check. Before the plan can be implemented, there may be real estate transactions that need to take place, trust agreements that need to be considered, life insurance considerations (including review of beneficiaries and other provisions), estate planning ramifications, and other important matters. Consider the various professionals who will be needed in order to successfully enact your financial plan: lawyers, accountants, etc. By involving key people at the beginning, it's much more likely that all the necessary legal instruments can be coordinated to raise the chance of a plan's overall success.

One of the benefits our firm provides is our strategic relationships with other professionals in the tax, legal, and financial services industries—relationships that we can leverage for our clients' benefit in order to help them make these necessary arrangements. We also work with advisors with whom the client already has long-standing, trusted relationships. Whichever type of advisor the client prefers, all the necessary legal instruments and understandings should be in place by the time we come to the commitment meeting.

Committing to your plan. The act of signing on the dotted line—making the real financial commitment to your overall investing plan—can be highly emotional. These emotions can be an investor's biggest weakness. Emotions can make us sellers when we ought to be buyers, and they can cause us to abandon the market when we ought to be patient.

Sometimes the step of committing to a new investment strategy can bring up emotions of fear and uncertainty. I structure my financial advisory process to minimize these negative emotions by ensuring that before we get to the commitment step, we've already made a thorough assessment of goals and dreams and have constructed a plan that is precisely calibrated to the investor's stage in life, risk tolerance, and objectives. We have done all of this based upon careful reasoning, time-tested financial research, and meticulous consideration of the client's needs.

Remember what Art Turock said: "When you're committed to something, you accept no excuses, only results." I suggest that you should also not accept fears, anxieties, and mental obstacles. If you've followed the process outlined so far, then you should have a rational understanding of how your investments will work together in the plan to reach your financial goals, and you should be able to take the step of commitment with confidence. If you still have questions that need answering about how your plan will be implemented, then by all means stop to answer these before going forward.

The specific mechanics of committing to a financial plan deserve a mention in and of themselves. There may be brokerage agreements to execute, accounts to fund, revised legal documents to authorize, and other paperwork necessary to establish your new plan. The documentation can be daunting and confusing, making it especially important to keep copies of everything and ask questions about anything you don't understand when signing on the dotted line.

Challenges to your commitment. As my clients make their commitment to their plans and as I make my commitment to them as their wealth advisor, I make it a point to name possible obstacles and challenges we may face while the investment plan is in motion. Inevitably, obstacles and difficulties will arise, and it's at the commitment stage that I encourage my clients to think about any circumstances that could challenge their commitment to their plan. I believe that a challenge that can be foreseen is also a challenge that can be overcome.

In Dorothy's case, for example, we considered her age and relevant life cycle factors, with a special focus on how health changes might come to bear in the future and require us to significantly alter the plan we'd both committed to. With Jake, on the other hand, we needed to consider a different set of potential challenges to his financial success: his younger age and the length of time he would need his money to be working for him, his need for budgeting discipline so as to avoid overspending, the near-term expenses of his education, and his medium-term goal of buying a house. Anticipating possible challenges, we built a number of assessment meetings into Jake's overall plan to make sure that we would be aware early on if any of these obstacles became a significant barrier to his continued commitment.

There are circumstances that can force you to reconsider and even to strategically alter your investment plan. The key word in that sentence, however, is "strategically." It is almost always a mistake to allow temporary mishaps or events force sweeping changes in your investment strategy. But when such events do arise—long-term shifts in market characteristics, fundamental changes in tax or financial laws that affect your holdings, sudden increases or decreases in the value of portions of your portfolio, life circumstances such as bereavement, divorce, or illness that alter the assumptions on which your plan is based—it is important to meet with your financial advisor to work systematically through the implications of these events and to consider how your financial plan may need to be adapted in response. In the next chapter, we'll discuss how to perform ongoing assessments that are required to ensure mutual commitment to the plan, and thus to continue moving in the direction of your goals.

WHEN ADJUSTMENTS ARE NEEDED

Of course, the financial markets are fluid and cyclical. Interest rates go up and down, stock prices rise and fall, industry groups go in and out of favor. Not only do the markets shift and change, but economic and tax policies also change, altering the favorability and advantages of various types of investments.

Therefore, every financial plan should be subject to ongoing assessment and fine-tuning to ensure that the overall strategy is still being implemented as it was designed. That is why I encourage all my clients, as we are making the commitment and beginning to implement the investment plan, to consider how they will approach the minor adjustments that are inevitably needed in every journey toward financial success. I ask them to think about any questions that arise in terms of how their investments are being handled and to bring these questions to the follow-up meetings that we schedule at preplanned intervals throughout the coming months and years.

STEP 1: DISCOVERING AND SETTING YOUR GOALS

- **What are my needs?** (family obligations, debt commitments, lifestyle requirements)
- **What are my desires?** (difference between a need and a desire)
- **Where do I want to go?** (life goals and relationship to financial goals; short-, mid-, and long-term goals)
- **When is it time to review or revise my goals?**

STEP 2: PLANNING YOUR INVESTMENTS

- **Do I know the fundamentals of investing?**
- **What does my asset allocation currently look like?**
- **What does diversification mean?**
- **Why shouldn't I try to time the market?**
- **What types of risk can I tolerate?**

STEP 3: COMMITTING TO YOUR PLAN

- **How do I enact my plan?**
- **How do I commit to that plan?**
- **What problems might challenge my commitment?**

ASSESSING YOUR PLAN

WOULDN'T LIFE BE great if all our plans went exactly as we envisioned, all our decisions were correct, and all our assumptions always held up? In such a perfect world, there would be no second-guessing, no Monday-morning quarterbacks, no regrets, and no need for assessment or reevaluation.

Of course, we don't live in that world. In our world change is the only constant, and even in those situations where we make appropriate decisions based on sound assumptions, circumstances have a way of changing. At that point, we must call our assumptions into question. That's why every financial plan needs to include periodic assessments, the fourth step in our five-step plan for financial success.

WHEN REVIEW IS NEEDED

Without a mechanism in place for periodic, systematic assessment of your portfolio and investment strategy, you run the risk of going off the road toward your goals and running into one of two ditches. Either you'll blindly assume that everything is going to be fine and miss the opportunity to make a needed adjustment at the right time, or you'll be constantly at the mercy of the ups and downs inherent to the financial markets and change investment directions based on "gut feelings" rather than on reasoned assessment. Neither of these is a recipe for financial success.

In my financial advising practice, we build regular, mutually agreed upon client meetings into the process so that we can review the financial plan and investments to make sure they are still the right match for the client's goals and life situation. Part of the reason we make this our fourth step is just good customer service: clients want to know that someone is watching out for their interests, that they're not just an account number among other account numbers. Questions also come up over time, especially if you have a number of different investment accounts that can be confusing to track. Knowing that you have a scheduled time to sit down, ask whatever questions you need to, and get a careful explanation can be a big relief.

If I've done a good job of listening and revealing all of my client's relevant goals and desires, and if I've carefully matched the client's level of risk tolerance and life cycle characteristics to the appropriate investment design, then the assessment process becomes a periodic review and recap of basic strategy, along with any needed rebalancing of the portfolio due to market action. As I said, the crucial determinants of portfolio performance are asset allocation and diversification, not market timing. Value-add portfolio management is about allowing historical and mathematical market principles to work over time. The proper assessment process ensures that these principles are still working with your basic financial situation as it stands—it is not about jumping in and out of investments and depleting your assets over time.

ARE YOU LISTENING?

Just as investors must commit to their plan and overall strategy, for the plan to achieve the most efficient results, they must also participate in regular, systematic assessment and heed the advice that comes out of that process.

Value-add portfolio management is about allowing historical and mathematical market principles to work over time. The proper assessment process ensures that these principles are still working with your basic financial situation as it stands.

Client Correspondence

In my financial advising practice, once we've gained the client's commitment and initiated the investment plan, we typically send out a letter that goes something like this:

> Dear Dorothy,
>   As you may be aware, you are now fully invested in a balanced portfolio. And may I add my personal congratulations on joining the elite group of individuals who have taken control and embraced their own financial destiny.
>   Again, my congratulations.
>   Kind regards,
>   Kimberly Foss, CFP®, CPWA®

I will also often include a memo itemizing the client's current holdings in his or her new investment plan. A sample memo might look something like this:

> *I wanted to update you on purchases for the dollar-cost averaging into the market. See the following:*
>
> **EQUITIES:**
> • DFEOX—Dimensional Fund Advisors Core Equity
>   1 mutual fund–$100,000.00

- DFQTX—Dimensional Fund Advisors Core Equity 2 mutual fund–$90,500.00
- VYSVX—Vericimetry US Small Cap Value mutual fund–$75,500.00
- DFIEX—Dimensional Fund Advisors International Core Equity mutual fund–$55,500.00

FIXED INCOME:

- DFIHX—Dimensional Fund Advisors One-Year Fixed Income mutual fund–$110,000.00
- Vanguard Utility Fund–$104,000.00

In the period between initiating a new investment strategy and the first sixty-day follow-up meeting, the client often experiences buyer's remorse. It's a great deal of money to have invested, after all, and it's natural for clients to doubt their previous conviction and wonder whether their plan is really the right thing to do. There can be uncertainties about the investment process and the asset allocation model generally, or memory may be hazy about fees or specific administrative aspects of the plan. Thus I send the "fully invested" letter and memo of current investment allocations as a reminder that a plan is in place and that it has been enacted to achieve his or her stated goals. I include basic information about what the plan includes in terms of dollar holdings in each investment. This letter puts a positive sense of expectation in place for the sixty-day review, when I will once again go over the fundamentals of the investment plan and revisit why he or she made the decision to go forward.

DON'T BE YOUR OWN WORST ENEMY!

One of the most important things I do during the initial follow-up meeting (which I generally hold at sixty days after the commitment meeting) is to remind clients of how we've designed their portfolios and the proven principles on which that design is based. In other words, I tell them—as many times as I have to—about efficient portfolio design and value-add management.

Why do I put such emphasis on value-add management at this stage of the process? Because invariably, sixty days after investing their assets, some current piece of news in the financial markets will have spooked the client. They either become convinced that our asset allocation model is wrong and that we're not correctly diversified, or that their investment plan needs to change immediately, with some investment dumped and replaced with whatever seems the most viable according to whatever news they've heard.

Most of us are not wired to withstand the emotional ups and downs of the markets. Absent the guidance and steadying influences of a disciplined investment strategy and a seasoned wealth advisor, most individual investors (and even some institutional ones!) fall victim to the classic greed/fear cycle, to their financial harm.

To help understand the emotions of investing and why most investors systematically make the wrong decisions, let's look for a moment at what happens when an investor gets a hot tip on a stock.

Most investors have experienced losing money on an investment—and did not enjoy that situation—so it's unlikely that any investor is going to race out and buy the stock immediately. Instead, a typical investor might follow it for a while to see how it does.

When the stock starts to trend upward, he starts to get excited. This time, things might be different; this might be the one investment that helps him make a lot of money. As the stock continues its upward trend, that hope turns firmly into greed, and he decides to buy the stock that day.

You know what happens next. As soon as the transaction clears,

the stock starts to go down and the investor feels a new combination of emotions, including fear and regret. He's made a terrible
mistake, and promises himself that if the stock just goes back up to
the level it was when he bought it, he will sell it and never buy like
this again. The desire to make money on a hot tip is gone; all he
wants now is a chance to undo the mistake without having to tell
his significant other about the money he's spent.

As the stock continues to trend down, the investor starts to feel
a new emotion—panic. And he sells the stock just as new information comes out and the stock races to an all-time high.

I've seen this cycle enacted scores of times over my years in
this business. Most of us are poorly wired for investing. Emotions are powerful forces that cause us to do exactly the opposite
of what we should do. Emotions lead us to buy high and sell low.
If we do that over a long period of time, we'll cause serious damage not just to our portfolio but also, more important, to our
financial dreams.

Wall Street has lots of great sayings, including, "If everybody

The Emotional Curve of Investing

THE EMOTIONAL CURVE OF INVESTING. SOURCE: CEG WORLDWIDE AND EMPYRION WEALTH
MANAGEMENT (WWW.EMPYRIONWEALTH.COM)

knows it, it's wrong or it's too late." The saying suggests that the "insiders" are the ones who benefit from all the hot tips and the rest of us don't find out about them—or act upon them—until it's too late. But the problem with this nugget of conventional Wall Street wisdom is that it feeds into the greed/fear cycle I've just described by propagating the mirage that somewhere there is hidden knowledge, and that the possessor of that knowledge holds the key to untold wealth. We all know that there are laws against trading based on insider knowledge. Just ask Martha Stewart or Enron's Kenneth Lay. Trying to get rich by cashing in on stock market rumors or the latest hot penny stock is just as likely to succeed as chasing a pot of gold at the end of the rainbow. And worse: it could cost you most or all of the gold you already have.

Here's another proverb that goes back to my training days at Merrill Lynch: "It is very difficult to make accurate predictions—especially about the future." While this might seem a merely humorous understatement, it does correctly frame the truth that basing

Timing

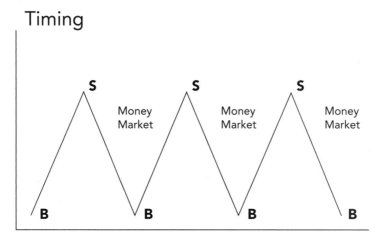

B = Buy: 100% invested in market when prices rise.
S = Sell: 100% invested in Money Market as prices fall.

your investment behavior on what pundits are promoting online and in the financial media is a notoriously unreliable strategy. It's not that there isn't worthwhile information out there; the problem is that if you restructure your holdings every time some new trend or stock idea shows up on *CNNMoney*, the only person who's going to get rich is the trader placing your buy/sell orders. Instead, you need a sound, disciplined approach that takes advantage of time-tested, proven investment strategies that can keep you on course for your goals, whether you're in a good market or a bad one.

To bear this out, take a look at the graphic on the following page. As the chart notes, missing the best twenty-five trading days since 1970 would have significantly cut the S&P 500 Index annualized compound return. Do you believe that you can time the market so perfectly that you will be in the market during every one of those ten days and out of it when the downdrafts occur?

This is what I characterized in chapter two as "investment pornography"—information that titillates us with the prospect of large returns, but that ultimately adds no real, long-term value. As I said, the goal of so many of the rumors and stories in the financial media and elsewhere is to motivate somebody, somewhere to generate a transaction—to buy or sell something. And why is that? Simply stated, much of the financial industry is still inherently a transaction-based enterprise. As I've already said and will say again, I believe that the client is best served when, instead of being paid a commission for executing an individual transaction, the financial advisor is paid a flat fee based on the overall value of the assets under management. I do see hopeful signs that the industry is moving in the fee-based direction. Nevertheless, about 70 percent of the business is still, in some way, transaction based. It's a way of thinking and an orientation to a business model that is deeply ingrained in the financial services culture, and it will take some time to see this change to the degree that it needs to change.

Performance of the S&P 500 Index
Daily: January 1, 1970–December 31, 2011

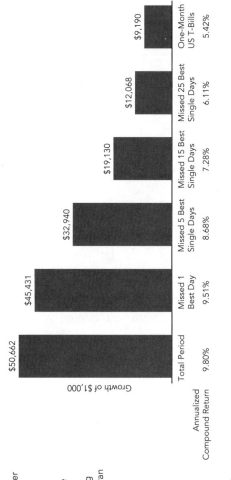

Growth of $1,000

	Total Period	Missed 1 Best Day	Missed 5 Best Single Days	Missed 15 Best Single Days	Missed 25 Best Single Days	One-Month US T-Bills
	$50,662	$45,431	$32,940	$19,130	$12,068	$9,190
Annualized Compound Return	9.80%	9.51%	8.68%	7.28%	6.11%	5.42%

The best single day was October 13, 2008.

The best one-month return, October 1974, happened immediately after the second-worst one-year period.

The occurrence of strongly positive returns has been especially unpredictable. Investors attempting to wait out an apparent downturn ran a high risk of missing these best periods.

Nine of the top 25 days occurred between September 2008 and February 2009, during which time the S&P dropped 41.8%

Five of the top 10 days occurred between October 2008 and November 2008, during which time, the S&P 500 dropped 21.5%.

So how can you escape the cycle of emotion-driven, rumor-chasing investing that will ultimately defeat your purpose? The answer is what we've been talking about throughout this book: first, have a carefully designed plan based on asset allocation and diversification and commit to that plan, and then practice the ongoing discipline of systematic evaluation and assessment, preferably with a financial professional. In short, stay the course. Instead of worrying about being "in" or "out" of the market at the right times, allow regular assessments to reveal any adjustments you need to make based on overall market conditions along the way. My goal for my clients is not to "get in" and "get out" at the right times, but rather to choose the correct asset allocation model for each client, to diversify the holdings appropriately in each asset class, and then to stay in for the long haul until the client reaches his or her goal.

It's true that adjustments to a portfolio design may become necessary. But any serious change to the overall market or to an investor's personal situation that might require major adjustments in the investor's portfolio design will be much more obvious than a fleeting hot tip. If an investor follows the discipline of regular assessments, he or she can make whatever adjustments need to be made on the basis of reasoned thinking rather than the fear/greed cycle, which allows the portfolio to do its work.

ASSESSMENT BASICS

Here are some questions you need to ask yourself and your financial advisor as you move into the assessment phase of your financial plan.

Q: What indicators do I look at to determine how well my plan is working?

A: With so much information available, how do you know what to pay attention to? How can you tell what areas of your portfolio you need to focus on—and how exactly do those areas work together to keep your financial vessel on course?

I believe that one of the most valuable services we provide to our clients is to help them get organized. We ask the client to bring all of his or her new account paperwork, statements, and other financial documents to the sixty-day follow-up meeting, along with any questions about the execution of the financial plan. At this meeting, we provide a notebook and help clients put all of their documents and statements in a logical order that is designed to help them feel more in control of their financial strategy. We answer questions until the client feels comfortable in his or her knowledge of how the money is being handled, along with how our strategy and portfolio design fits in with the client's overall goals and needs.

Once we have created organization, it's time to review other aspects of the portfolio and the underlying investment strategy.

Q: Is my asset allocation properly balanced?

A: We design and implement the investment plan for our clients, selling and buying securities as needed to position the client's holdings in accordance with the asset allocation and diversification model we've established. However, over time, the relative weightings of assets in the portfolio will shift because of interest earned and any appreciation or depreciation in the value of the holdings. When this occurs, the portfolio must be rebalanced in order to remain within the boundaries of the asset allocation model we have established.

Rebalancing. Some investment holdings will grow faster than others. Rebalancing ensures that your portfolio doesn't begin to overemphasize one or more asset categories due to changes in that rate of growth. Rebalancing to reassert the asset allocation model also ensures that your portfolio remains within the risk/return parameters that we established when we initially designed the plan.

Let's assume, for example, that we initially determined that equity investments should represent 60 percent of your portfolio. However, after a recent stock market increase, stock investments now represent 80 percent of your portfolio, because the stocks you own now have a higher real value relative to your other investments. To rebalance your asset allocation to the percentages called for in your model, you would need either to sell some of your stock investments or to purchase investments from an under-weighted asset category.

Rebalancing also involves reviewing the investments within each asset allocation category to maintain appropriate diversification. It's the same principle: if any holdings within the same asset category become unbalanced because of increases or decreases in the market value of a particular stock or bond, I will recommend changes to adjust them back to their original percentages within that asset category.

Our basic asset allocation model includes the percentages by which an asset class must become "out of plan" in order to precipitate rebalancing. The principal advantage of taking this preplanned approach to rebalancing is, of course, that it conforms to the timeless market adage of buying low and selling high. When an asset is overperforming, rebalancing tends to force us to capture the gains; when an asset is temporarily underperforming, rebalancing encourages us to purchase at a lower price and enjoy the eventual upside. By having our parameters established in advance, we avoid the emotional tendency to fall victim to the greed/fear cycle.

Investors ask at this point, "But why would I want to buy more of an underperforming asset? Why would I want more of a loser in my portfolio?" The answer is this: if we've designed your portfolio properly, you shouldn't have to pay attention to any particular individual asset, but rather to the overall mix. It's the asset mix and the broad diversification that is your best protection against volatility, not picking the right stocks or avoiding having more shares of a "loser." Strategic portfolio design and value-add management work mathematically and historically; picking stocks and trying to time the market generally results in a portfolio that bleeds red ink. We stay with the plan and do what it tells us; we don't listen to background "market noise" or make strategic decisions on the basis of what a single asset sector might be doing at the moment.

One thing to take into account when rebalancing is the transaction fees and tax consequences that may apply. Because I operate on a fee-only basis, the transaction fees my clients pay are very low, but we still review this and make sure clients understand exactly what it will cost them to bring their portfolios back into alignment with the overall plan design, and also whether the transactions will generate any taxable gains that must be reported.

Q: What's next on my wealth agenda?

A: The final question to ask about your assessment process is one that moves from the present state of your finances toward your future goals and the steps you need to take to achieve them. This is where the assessment process asks you once again to focus on your short-, medium-, and long-term goals so you can judge how your investment strategy is allowing you to progress toward them.

Here, we are less interested in any implications for specific holdings or actions within your portfolio than we are in helping you think about upcoming events, possibilities, and life-cycle changes that could impact your goals. In the same way that we want to make reasoned, preplanned decisions about the parameters for keeping your portfolio balanced, we also want to forecast future needs and desires to make sure that we have appropriate plans in place.

For my Gen Xer client Jake, this planning might involve considerations about future family plans. For Danny and Sandy, however, securing their grandchildren's college education was an important upcoming item on the agenda. Dorothy wanted to be able to leave a significant portion of her assets as an inheritance for her children, and Scott and Mary were interested in positioning their investments so that they could plan for an early and active retirement lifestyle. All needs and desires come with price tags, and my job as their wealth advisor is to begin looking to these future needs, to develop the practical investment strategies that can help meet those needs, and to make sure through the assessment process that the overall investment plan is on track to meet them. If it's not, then we need to make adjustments.

"BORN AGAIN"

Not long after I started my business, I wrote a guest article for a local newspaper. One of the people who had been in Certified Financial Planner classes with me read my article, called me up, and made a comment that led to my second major life-changing moment.

I had written about the importance of asset allocation—having your eggs in different types of baskets—and when George called, he said, "Kimberly, your article was great, and what you're doing is cutting-edge. But in the end, you're going to disappoint your clients."

"Why?" I asked. "I'm using asset allocation; I'm not charging transaction fees . . ."

"Yes," he said. "You are utilizing the concept of 'value-add' portfolio management, but you are using actively managed mutual funds, which are the wrong tools."

By value-add portfolio management, George meant that I wasn't trying to spot trends and buy or sell within the portfolios to maximize returns (active management). He was right. I was diversifying my "eggs" into different baskets by positioning my clients in various market segments, but I was using mutual funds and managers who believed in timing—the exact opposite of value-add investing. George went on to say, "You are doing right by your clients conceptually, but you're using the wrong tool. You are using a hammer and nails. What you need is a nail gun."

According to George, portfolio management firms were being set up to do on a large scale what I was doing on a very small scale, but using value-add portfolio structure. He went on to tell me about one of these portfolio management firms, a group called Dimensional Fund Advisors. He said they were putting on a seminar in the near future and recommended that I attend. I did.

What happened at that seminar was nothing less than a born-again experience. Within three minutes of hearing the opening remarks from Dan Wheeler, who presented on efficient portfolio design theory and the three-factor model, I realized that I had been doing value-add investing and portfolio management the hard way all along.

The more Dan spoke about portfolio efficiency, asset class investing, dissimilar price movement, diversification, and the relationship between risk and return, the more the concepts simply clicked, as if someone had flipped a light switch in my brain. What he was describing resonated so strongly with me that I knew I would never go back to the old way of investing my clients' assets and portfolios. I was now truly and irrevocably committed to efficient portfolio design—and I've been that way ever since.

ASSESSING MY OWN PLAN

As I moved forward with my wealth advising practice, I came more and more to appreciate the rationality of the portfolio design and the value-add management tools available to me through my new colleagues at Dimensional Fund Advisors. The new theories I was working with appealed to my need for structure and order—it was like studying architecture again, except now I was studying the architecture of investments. I was truly in my element and it showed in my practice. I began to attract an entirely new class of investors: engineers, scientists, doctors. In these fields, theories need to be precise and the data need to make logical sense. With my new investment philosophy, I not only had all the data anyone could ever want, but I had something based on proven theories of portfolio management, something that was logical, that clearly flowed from basic premises, and that was borne out by the data. I could talk to the engineers about my investment philosophy and they understood it; I could explain the concepts to surgeons and scientists, and they loved it. To this day, most of my clients come from among these groups.

Besides the solid theoretical foundations I was now using in designing portfolios, my new relationship with Dimensional Fund Advisors also gave me access to sophisticated tools that took so much of the guesswork out of financial planning. Instead of doing it the way I had done it before—basically using linear rates of returns as assumptions for my clients to estimate their retirement needs under various scenarios—I now was able to use the statistical analysis tools known collectively as the Monte Carlo Simulations to project the future value of a client's portfolio under various scenarios and to locate the point on the risk/return continuum where their investments would perform most efficiently. George had been right—by assessing my own goals and practices and then acting on them, I retired my hammer and nails (sorry, Dad) for a brand-new, high-powered, shiny nail gun. Now I was prepared!

I was now in a position to provide state-of-the-art investment management and advice. By helping my clients understand the benefits of modern portfolio theory and by using statistically

Action Point: Don't Be Scared; Be Prepared

Having a carefully designed investing strategy is the best anti-dote to the greed/fear cycle. When you know how your portfolio will perform in various market scenarios and when you build those understandings into your investment plan, you no longer have to fret about day-to-day market fluctuation. Also, when you have confidence in the foundational principles on which your portfolio is built, you are less inclined to yield to the temptation to do things that are counterproductive to your long-term goals.

But portfolio design also helps in another way: it allows you to make sound decisions about when you need to make adjustments to your portfolio. By modeling various scenarios, it is possible to formulate disciplined, logical plans as to when you should make changes in your investment approach. Once again, rather than operating on emotion, you are making choices based on proven principles. A professional, qualified investment advisor can help you put portfolio strategies into place that allow you to face the uncertain future in the market with confidence.

---

proven models, I was able to formulate clear and consistent reasons for the recommendations I made. I could also give clear guidance and assessment parameters, as well as reliable feedback on how we were doing on our journey toward the client's financial goals.

But as I've already said, in today's fast-moving financial markets, there is no autopilot setting. Unexpected events can occur that can knock the statistical models sideways. What that means is that besides being built on a sound theoretical foundation, an investment plan also must be designed with a certain amount of flexibility to survive and ultimately thrive in unusual market conditions when normal models cease to apply.

And as my clients and I would learn, the market conditions in October 2008 were some of the most unusual in history. We would find our flexibility tested to its maximum limits . . . as the final chapter will show.

STEP 1: DISCOVERING AND SETTING YOUR GOALS

- **What are my needs?** (family obligations, debt commitments, lifestyle requirements)
- **What are my desires?** (difference between a need and a desire)
- **Where do I want to go?** (life goals and relationship to financial goals; short-, mid-, and long-term goals)
- **When is it time to review or revise my goals?**

STEP 2: PLANNING YOUR INVESTMENTS

- **Do I know the fundamentals of investing?**
- **What does my asset allocation currently look like?**
- **What does diversification mean?**
- **Why shouldn't I try to time the market?**
- **What kinds of risk can I tolerate?**

STEP 3: COMMITTING TO YOUR PLAN

- **How do I enact my plan?**
- **How do I commit to that plan?**
- **What problems might challenge my commitment?**

STEP 4: ASSESSING YOUR PLAN

- **What indicators do I look at to determine how well my plan is working?**
- **Is my asset allocation properly balanced?**
- **What's next on my wealth agenda?**

KEEPING YOUR PLAN FLEXIBLE

IN 2004, NASSIM NICHOLAS TALEB, in his book *Fooled by Randomness*, first set forth his theory of what he called "Black Swan Events." Taleb named his theory after an expression that was common in eighteenth-century London to denote an event that was previously assumed to be impossible, but that happened anyway. In the Old World, all swans were assumed to be white. Thus, when black swans were discovered in Australia in 1697, what was previously assumed to be impossible was suddenly proven not only possible but true.

Taleb uses this metaphor as a way to address unexpected events in science, arts, history, or finance, and the impact these events can have on our lives and expectations. As Taleb defines his term, a Black Swan Event

1. is a surprise to the observer;

2. has a major impact; and

3. is subsequently rationalized as if it could have been anticipated or expected.

October 10, 2008, was a Black Swan Event. The catastrophic occurrences in the financial markets that led up to that historic market meltdown slammed into investors and finance professionals like a tidal wave. Billions of dollars in market capitalization were wiped out; many saw nearly a third of the value of their investments lopped off. People across the nation were starting to talk about the possibility of a second Great Depression.

The only way to avoid ruin was to find a new path forward. Since we were dealing with an unprecedented situation, we had to disregard—at least temporarily—much of the rule book. After all, in a Black Swan Event previous assumptions no longer apply. The only thing that could help an investor ride out the storm would be flexibility.

A SYSTEM ON THE BRINK

We've already discussed some factors that brought the market to the edge of disaster in 2008: the bursting of the real estate bubble, the toxic mortgage loans in bank portfolios, and the rampant greed that caused giant financial institutions to pursue greater and greater returns without regard to risk. But much of this background was essentially invisible to the average investor as we headed into the second half of 2008. Even when Lehman Brothers collapsed in September 2008, the structured CDs in my clients' portfolios were still paying the guaranteed interest as contracted.

But then the swelling current of financial mishaps began to erode the levees, and like the streets of New York during Hurricane Sandy, the market was inundated by disaster. Lehman's bankruptcy began a downward spiral that would wipe out trillions of dollars in global market capitalization within a month. Many firms that had been market stalwarts for years found themselves on the brink of financial collapse and were absorbed by bigger and better-capitalized competitors.

Earlier, JP Morgan Chase had purchased Bear Stearns at a fire sale price, while Merrill Lynch was on the block and would be absorbed into Bank of America. The state-owned Korea Development Bank had shied away from taking a stake in Lehman Brothers, which then looked to the UK-based Barclays PLC for a lifeline. Instead, Barclays abandoned plans to buy the entire firm, later swooping in after Lehman was left to fail, to buy the pieces, beginning with the distressed company's US units.

BREAKING THE BUCK

Unexpectedly caught in the domino effect was the Primary Fund, a giant among money market funds and a flagship enterprise of the Reserve Group, the financial powerhouse that had originally created money market funds as an asset class. Money market funds are designed to be the safest of investments. They typically invest in relatively low-risk securities such as US Treasury bills, CDs, and other highly liquid securities. By investing in and redeeming such short-term securities—sometimes holding an investment as briefly as overnight—the fund seeks to maintain the net asset value of each share at the relatively constant value of $1. But you, as an investor, get a higher rate of return than that which a typical checking or savings account makes available, a rate usually in the 3–6 percent range, depending on the interest rate environment.

But the assets of the money market fund, we soon learned, had significant exposure to Lehman's short-term debt, and in the wake of Lehman's collapse, those assets lost value. Consequently, the highly respected money market fund announced that their customers invested in money market accounts would lose money. Instead of getting a dollar back for every dollar they had invested, those who held shares in the money market fund could perhaps redeem them for $0.97 each. (Shares in its Caribbean fund were even lower, at $0.91.)

The unthinkable had happened—in the lexicon of Wall Street, the money market fund was "breaking the buck." It was only the second time in history that shares of a money market fund had fallen below $1 in value.

The money market fund's staggering announcement triggered a four-day, $142 billion run on institutional funds as worried investors fled *en masse* for the safety of government securities. Adding fuel to the fire was the decision by Boston-based Putnam Investments to close its $12.3 billion Putnam Prime Money Market Fund in the face of "significant redemption pressure." In short, there was a potential for a massive run on the bank.

The phrase "run on the bank" was coined during the days of the gold rush back in my home territory of California. Gold nuggets were heavy, hard to store, and difficult to secure, so the miners would deposit their gold at the local bank and would receive a paper receipt. When bandits would ride into town and stage a bank robbery, word spread quickly and everybody panicked. So as not to be left with worthless pieces of paper as their gold nuggets rode off into the sunset on someone else's horse, the townspeople would literally run to the bank to try to get their gold back. Thus, whether the robbers got the gold or not, the bank vault was often left empty.

This is essentially what happened in a single week of September 2008. The bad news on Wall Street triggered a stampede on Main Street. With a near panic on its hands, the government stepped in to prevent a financial catastrophe. It announced the $786 billion bailout plan known as the Troubled Asset Relief Program, or TARP. Thirteen banks were to be saved. Soon these were nick-named "Hank's Banks" in honor of Henry Paulson Jr., secretary of the Treasury. The financial world breathed a sigh of relief.

I was skeptical. This kind of bailout had occurred once before, during the Great Depression. At that time, the Federal Deposit Insurance Corporation had been signed into law to prevent bank runs. In my mind, the handwriting was on the wall.

WHEN YOU CAN'T WAKE UP FROM THE NIGHTMARE

Have you ever had a nightmare in which you are mortally fright-ened, and just at the moment something terrible is about to hap-pen, you wake up? What if you didn't wake up? What if you had to keep living in the nightmare?

In October 2008, our country's overwhelming financial night-mare deepened. US insurance giant AIG was teetering on the brink of bankruptcy after the major credit agencies downgraded its rat-ing. AIG had to raise $14.5 billion in extra collateral just to meet its obligations. Classifying AIG as "too big to fail," the US gov-ernment had given AIG an $85 billion bailout, and the company was already hitting up the New York Fed for more. In the wake of this earth-shaking news, Wall Street posted its worst single-day fall since 9/11. In the space of ten days, the S&P also had fallen 23 per-cent to 899.62, while across the pond, the global panic continued as London's FTSE 100 plunged below the 5,000 watermark for the first time in three years.

On October 10, 2008, I felt a sinking sense of doom. The finan-cial foundation was crumbling under the country's largest insurer, a global empire that had been built on providing safety and secu-rity to its customers. I remember thinking to myself, *The whole world just changed forever. It will never be the same.*

Yet as I stared out of my office to the street below, I was

astonished that life was going on as before. The doors of Starbucks were constantly in motion as people went in and out, hugging their lattes, Frappuccinos, and mochas. They were texting and chatting on their cell phones while picking up their dry cleaning. I recall observing a flower delivery to the building across the street from my office and thinking to myself, *Don't you all know what's happening out there? Who is sending flowers to someone on a day like today?* Did these people on the street not understand that the walls of their reality were already crumbling? The financial world was being reshaped forever, as if a giant meteor was hurtling on a direct collision course with earth, and I was the only one aware of the impending doom. I felt like one of those apocalyptic prophets in the movies crying, "The end is near!" But this wasn't a movie—this was reality.

Across the board, financial companies were facing sharply lower profits. Goldman Sachs alone had reported a 70 percent drop in profits. There was a credit freeze, as banks no longer trusted each other enough to make loans, lest some toxic assets bring the house down. The government was not forthcoming with adequate solutions, and Wall Street financiers and investment bankers were busily blaming each other. As if all this weren't bad enough, the country of Iceland went bankrupt. This crisis had the power to wipe out the financial integrity of an entire nation! What would happen next?

Yes, I saw the meteor coming that day: Friday, October 10. It was the start of the longest, darkest weekend of my life. How was I going to save my clients amid the worst global financial meltdown in history? This calamity, brought on by greed and hubris on the part of powerful financial executives, was unprecedented; ahead of me stretched uncharted territory. How could I possibly figure out what to do for my clients, the people who had trusted me to manage their assets and to take care of them?

Could I depend on the US government or a financial power-house to save the day? Pounding over and over in my brain was this thought: *Someone has to do something to bring us out of this.* I remember literally falling down to my knees, palms together in prayer, asking God for help to save my clients. They were depending on me, and I was out of answers.

On Monday, the chaos continued. The once-familiar cast of Wall Street characters was rapidly changing. Shotgun marriages were being hastily arranged to save large financial institutions from keeling over. Bank of America bought Merrill Lynch, the nation's largest retail brokerage, for $50 billion. With its back broken by punitive mortgage-related losses, Washington Mutual (WAMU), one of the country's largest banks with $307 billion in assets, was seized by the Fed and sold to JPMorgan Chase. At the time of sale, WAMU's stock price had fallen 95 percent, from a year's high of $36.47 to $1.69.

On a landscape littered with the corpses of competitors, only two investment banks were left standing, and those just barely. One was an old-school elite leader in investment banking, and the other was a spinoff from a well-established bank that had been created when the 1933 Glass-Steagall Act mandated separation between commercial and investment banks.

There were two banks still standing in a year that had started with five.

BANKS AND TARP

At the time, an investment bank could leverage each dollar of its capital forty-two times. By comparison, a commercial bank like Bank of America could leverage the same capital only six times. Imagine being in Las Vegas and having the power to bet every one-dollar chip you have forty-two times. You would certainly lose a few bets, but some of these could likely turn out to be big winners that would help you cover your losses and then some.

As an investment bank, you can win big, as everyone did during the dotcom boom. But when you lose, you are left with less than nothing—not only is your capital gone, but you also have the debt incurred from using the leverage—essentially, spending money that you did not have. In contrast, a commercial bank must take less risky bets; it can only leverage its dollar six times. But these safer bets are insured, and while a bank might still lose all its investments, it can only lose what it has actually put in.

"Hank's Banks," as the lot of them were referred to at the time, were beset by plunging share prices and a collapse in public confidence. At this point in the financial meltdown, the safety of staid commercial banking sounded like the best deal in town. And these commercial banks could boost their resources by getting access to TARP money. Thus they caved in and converted from investment banks to a more highly regulated, lower-risk commercial bank charter. Basically, they were exchanging oversight by the Securities and Exchange Commission for the more rigorous scrutiny of the Federal Reserve and several other government agencies.

The Fed rushed its approval, waiving the five-day waiting period, and the two investment banks became bank-holding companies overnight. Now they had to conform to the rules of commercial banks, which meant that they first had to write off all of their debt and beef up their capital ratios to satisfy commercial banking requirements.

On Monday morning, the headlines screamed, "America's largest banks in need of liquidity." TARP funding had yet to be released, and the banks were scrambling to pay off what they owed. Once again, the thought that had dominated my weekend surfaced: *Someone has to do something.*

Someone did. Warren Buffett, the world's richest man in 2008, bought a chunk of one bank for $5 billion through his company, Berkshire Hathaway. Buffett received $5 billion in stock with a generous 10 percent yield and another $5 billion in warrants to buy shares of preferred stock at $115 a share, $10 below the closing price when the deal was announced. It was a life raft that was difficult to refuse.

Now only one of Hank's Banks remained standing alone in the breach, trying to figure out how to bridge the gap between its balance sheet and TARP funding. No one knows what was going on internally, but what appeared to be the answer was something called kiting.

All of us have done it from time to time: putting a check in the mail on Monday, knowing that money would be deposited into the account on Tuesday, and hoping that the bank will make the funds available by the time the utility company cashes the check on Wednesday.

No one can know for sure on the outside, but it is thought that this was what the bank was doing: writing checks against incoming TARP funds. The problem was that the TARP money was not flowing in as speedily as hoped, stuck as it was in government bureaucracy. US taxpayers had vehemently protested against the unprecedented bank bailout, and TARP squeaked through both houses of Congress only by a very slim margin.

A large Japanese banking giant, the second-largest bank in the world, had previously stepped in to take a 21 percent stake in the bank for $9 billion. It was not a smooth and easy transaction, and the Japanese bank sought to renegotiate the deal when the bank lost half its value after its share price plummeted in October. Finally, the Japanese investor settled on buying preferred shares with a 10 percent dividend, an agreement structured similarly to the Buffett investment in the other bank. The US government also got in on the act, buying $10 billion in the bank's preferred shares as part of its plan to bolster the capital base of the troubled bank.

These transactions had slowed the bleeding, but they hadn't stopped it.

It appeared the bank needed extra money immediately to stay afloat until it received the TARP funds. If the company could not gain sufficient liquidity, it might not survive, and the TARP money would arrive too late to do any good. Once again, someone had to do something.

But this time, that someone would be the free markets: a once-in-a-lifetime opportunity for my clients!

THE PHONE CALL THAT CHANGED EVERYTHING

At this point, I was on my knees at two in the morning praying for a miracle. And as is often the case, it is in the darkest hour when the light shines the brightest. The light wrapped me like a warm blanket in delivering the answer to my prayers. It arrived as a phone call from one of my independent bond brokers and my longtime friend, William (one of the best bond brokers I have had the privilege to work with, I might add). Through the years, William and I had worked together to locate solid individual bond opportunities for my clients, often with more favorable coupon rates and maturities than the ones available through the usual sources. Many of the investment banks and financial institutions that were in the news now had been offering us favorable rates based upon structured certificates of deposit. (See the case study on Dorothy in chapter two for an example.) As a result of his work, William was constantly in touch with many of the nation's largest financial institutions.

Today, William was calling because he had just had a conversation with a close contact of his at one of Hank's Banks.

"Kimberly, how much money can you get together for an investment in one of Hank's Banks?"

"How much do you need?"

"Whatever you can provide."

"First things first. What kind of investment are they offering?"

He paused for a few seconds. "Make it up," he said.

"What?" I nearly dropped the phone. "Excuse me, what did you just say?"

"I said you can make up whatever investment vehicle you want. My contact at the bank says they're waiting for their TARP funds, but they need cash—basically a bridge loan—and they need it as quickly as possible. So my contact says to just get them some money, design your own investment vehicle, and they will get it approved."

In a month of staggering and incredible revelations, nothing I had heard on the news or read in the newspapers shocked me as much as his statement did. This was unheard of.

Because of the bank's urgent need for cash, I was being handed the opportunity to custom-design a financial product.

To put this in context: when designing new financial products, Wall Street hires some of the brightest and best. Any one of them would give his or her eyeteeth for an opportunity like this, just once in a career. That opportunity had just fallen into my lap.

Here was the answer to my prayers, the opportunity to do the right thing for my clients and help the free markets in a small way as well. My alpha-female, hunter-hero persona immediately kicked in. Although I did not have the slightest idea what kind of investment I was going to create, intuitively, I did have the sense that it could be big.

NOT IN KANSAS ANYMORE

At that moment, I went from being a small-town wealth advisor to becoming a quasi-investment banker for a key player in the world's biggest financial crisis.

How was I going to make this work? I was not some black-box genius who made a career out of dreaming up exotic financial investments, by any stretch of the imagination.

My thoughts flashed to my clients. They trusted me with their entire financial worth, in most cases, and they depended on my guidance to get them through this financial chaos. But I knew one thing: at the core, my clients had no doubt that whatever I did, it would first and foremost be in their best interest, as I had always demonstrated in the past twenty-five years. Now, one of Hank's Banks was asking the same. In the face of the enormity of the situation, one thought flashed into my mind: *I don't think we're in Kansas anymore.*

It was an odd thing to think. One of Hank's Banks had just asked me to come up with a way to use my clients' money to provide the cash they needed immediately, and the first thing that came to my mind was a quote from *The Wizard of Oz*? It was then that the light bulb flashed. Dorothy, my client, and the structured CDs that were created for her in 2007!

I ran over to my filing cabinet (yes, I still keep paper copies of important ideas), yanked it open, scrabbled through the folders, and pulled out Dorothy's portfolio. The structured CD that was devised to invest her inheritance would not be exactly what was needed, but it was the genesis of an idea, and I knew it was the right place to start the process.

The end objectives would be the same as they had been when we had been seeking a way to answer Dorothy's concerns about the security of her investment. I was looking for some immediate "drip" on our investment with a significant long-term income potential.

I also needed the money to be guaranteed (in some fashion) so as to provide safety for my clients. I wanted to buy the investment at a discount (always looking for a deal, even in a crisis), and I wanted to structure it with a death put option so that if any of my clients passed away, their portfolio assets would immediately be made available to their beneficiaries. (The death put option allows the beneficiary to sell the bond back to the issuer. It's also known as a survivor's option.) But most important, above anything else, I had to be absolutely and positively sure that—since my clients were in essence extending a loan to the bank—they would be paid back first, before any other creditor.

In the event of a corporate bankruptcy, the unwinding process observes a strict protocol as to the order in which creditors and others get paid as the company's assets are being liquidated. When there is not enough money for everyone, certain creditors are first in line to be repaid.

The debt that takes priority over all others is *senior debt*. A senior note holder gets paid off first, before the junior debt, the preferred stockholders, the unsecured creditors, or the shareholders of the common stock, the last having only a residual claim.

I called William back. "How about creating a senior note?" I asked.

Over the next twenty-four hours, William and I mapped out the concept of a senior note for the bank and then cherry-picked and inserted those features that represented the best attributes of various investments I had worked with. At each and every turn, I asked myself, *Will this provision benefit my clients?* If it did not, the idea was immediately discarded. If it did, I worked out a way to include it in a manner that the bank could accept.

For example, the structured CDs I had worked on in the past were wonderful little tools, but I disliked the one-year call option that I had been asked to include in exchange for the higher rate of return. It was too disruptive to my clients' income flow and did not provide the necessary longevity of income. Since I was creating this product from the ground up, I decided to insert a call date that was three years out. I figured that the rest of 2008 would be ugly, and 2009 would be difficult as the tattered financial system picked up the pieces. But I hoped that by 2010 or 2011, we would start to see some normalcy and growth in the economy. If two years would be enough time for some improvement, three years would be a bit more on the safe side, which is what I wanted for my clients.

This kind of note would not have the capital protection that the FDIC afforded. But I also knew that short-term securities like the one I was creating could be reinsured by another government program called the Temporary Liquidity Guarantee Program (TLGP), a program developed to promote liquidity during the darkest hours of the credit crisis. The TLGP insurance was a temporary program set to expire in 2012, so the three-year call date was also within the time frame of its protection.

At some point in the early hours of the morning—after having gone back and forth fleshing out the concept with William, who, in turn, had to present it to his contact at the bank—I decided to ask for the moon. I set the interest payment at 15 percent for a fifteen-year maturity date, retaining the three-year call option. If the note wasn't redeemed at the three-year call date, it would then be treated as a fifteen-year debt, but the bank had the right to redeem the note at face value on a quarterly basis. Conversely, if the note was never called, at the end of the fifteen years, my clients would receive 100 percent of the principal they'd invested, plus 15 percent interest paid monthly.

It was a bold call. Warren Buffet's deal had paid him 10 percent; I was asking for 15. By my reasoning, though, it was just like any important purchase negotiation—by asking for slightly more than

I thought I could get, I would be more likely to end up with the investment I wanted.

In the end, the bank agreed to everything but the 15 percent rate. We settled on 10.75 percent—three-quarters of a percent better than Warren Buffett's deal, I might add.

Once everything was approved, I knew that this was more than a home run; this was a grand slam in the bottom of the ninth inning of the World Series of the entire financial universe. William and I were thrilled. But the professional pride I felt was subsumed by the certainty that I had taken care of my clients in the best way possible.

Like everyone in the stock market at that time, some of my clients saw paper losses in their portfolios, but through diversification and commitment to their investment plans, their portfolios' temporary dips were not nearly as large as those experienced by the rest of the world. Additionally, by structuring this senior note investment, I had built a bridge to normalcy and better times ahead for my clients. The big Wall Street firms had taken a series of devastating hits, and I knew that retail investors would be next, but it would take a while for the massive losses to trickle down to them. There are several degrees of separation between Wall Street players and the man on the street who would neither understand the ramifications of the crisis nor feel the impact on his wallet until several months later. Nevertheless, the consequences of the ugly events that were taking place on Wall Street would soon spill over to the outside world. When the flood waters started to rise on Main Street, the bridge I had constructed for my clients would see them safely across to protection and security. I remember feeling as if I had just invented the life raft when the *Titanic* was sinking, and I had enough rafts for everyone on board!

But the celebratory feeling was still premature. For the plan to work, I had to communicate the concept to each and every one of my clients. I had to allay their fears and get the message across that this investment would work out nicely for them at a time when the financial landscape wasn't looking like a very nice place. The success of my plan and the bank's urgent need for funding hung in the balance, so I needed to clearly communicate with my clients what I knew from the depths of my being: that this was the bridge over troubled waters for their portfolios.

"FOLLOW THE FEDERAL BRICK ROAD"

I had over eighty clients, and I had only a short weekend to ensure proper allocations in their portfolio, present the proposal to them, and get their approval.

Time was pressing hard because I knew that if I didn't complete this transaction before the bank would receive TARP funds, or the urgency would be gone and the whole idea would die on the vine. I did not have time to reach my clients individually on the phone as I normally do.

On Saturday and Sunday, I went carefully through each of my client's portfolios. I tailored their participation in the bank investment in a way that fit their risk profiles and their investment goals and objectives. For some of my clients, a fifty-fifty split between equity and fixed income was appropriate. There were others who were in a later stage of their lives, and for these clients, a thirty-seventy asset mix weighted toward fixed income was more prudent. This variance among the portfolios meant that I had to break up my proposal into customized investments that would be appropriate for each of my clients. It took a while to get the math to work the way it needed to in order to figure out the proper division, but I was not going to compromise on the efficiency of my clients' portfolios by creating a "one size fits all" vehicle that would favor some clients over others. Sure enough, it took me most of Saturday night to work out the clients' portfolios and the different sets of figures that would make up the proposal to the bank.

That entire weekend I worked nonstop, and I tailored an e-mail for each of my clients explaining the bank proposal, what the senior note was and how it would work for them, and what they could expect from the investment moving forward. I am proactive in my advice to my clients and they are accustomed to receiving communications from me via phone calls, e-mails, or letters that propose ideas on what to do next with their investments *before* implementing those ideas. This idea was no different, and my individualized e-mail would not have come as a surprise to very many of my clients.

In the normal course of business, an e-mail with an investment proposal for one of my clients would close with a sentence like this: "Please consider this opportunity and contact me at your convenience to discuss whether it is an appropriate investment for your portfolio." But this e-mail was different. It stressed the urgency of the situation and explained that *unless I heard otherwise* from them within three days, I would assume that they had each given me tacit approval to go ahead with their participation in this investment.

Because of their trust in me, most of my clients were willing to give me the thumbs-up on the deal. But several were unnerved by the dire predictions and doom-and-gloom sound bites in the media. It was hard to blame them for this; after all, at this point in time, Wall Street was no longer recognizable. The elite investment banks no longer existed and there had been a massive run on money market funds. If cash was no longer safe, where could they invest their money?

Of course, at the top of my list of clients who would require personal assurance was the one who had given me the idea for the senior note in the first place: Dorothy.

TALKING TO DOROTHY

Again, Dorothy had grown up during the Great Depression; she had seen her parents suffer through bank closures and unemployment. To her, the current teetering financial environment was all too familiar; this was what she had been afraid of all along. She wanted to know, first and foremost, how safe her money would be if she followed my recommendation.

I explained to her why positioning her in the bank note was the best possible strategy at this point in time for her. I explained that this was a "structured investment" and that it carried risk. I had, however, scoured through the pros and cons, and despite the financial storm, this was a good investment for a portion of her portfolio. I further assured her that I was investing my own money as well. Something I could state about this investment that I couldn't say about the high-flying stocks we were "encouraged" to sell in my days in the brokerage industry was that this time, I *would* have invested my mother's money.

But Dorothy still needed more education, so I explained detailed workings of the note, the nuts and bolts of what held it together and why. Dorothy peppered me with questions, and it soon became apparent that the bulk of her concerns centered on the lack of capital protection from the FDIC. She needed an assurance that should anything go wrong—if the bank entered bankruptcy, for example—that she would be able to retrieve all her capital. She really had trouble comprehending the wisdom in putting her money in anything that wasn't federally insured (not that I could blame her at that time).

I did my best to assure her that I did not think the bank would fail. I explained to her that the promised TARP money could be available from the government by the end of the week. I also explained how the TLGP insurance worked on issuances of some debt investments by banks. More important, this bank had received capital infusions from two powerful parties—the US government and Japan's largest bank! It would be highly unlikely that such a global union would result in failure, although yes, they still could fail. I recalled one of my educational phone calls to her in the past: "risk and reward" are related, and that is why you get paid in the capital markets for taking that risk.

"Be in bed with the Fed," I told Dorothy, "and follow the federal brick road. That's what we're doing. The US government is the safest place to be right now. They're taking action to make sure that the banks make it through this crisis, and this opportunity puts us right alongside them."

Then I revealed the best part. "In fact, because this is a senior note," I said, "we get paid back first. The US government and other global banks invest their assets in the form of preferred stock. That means that even though they have put in the lion's share of the money, if the bank is in jeopardy of bankruptcy and funds are made available to repaying investors, you will get your money back *before all the others, due to your investment in a senior note.* You are first in line."

I could hear the sigh of relief in Dorothy's voice on the phone; she felt safe.

My clients agreed to go ahead because my conviction was unshakable that this investment was a sound strategy for them. I knew without a shred of doubt that this was a once-in-a-lifetime opportunity and that it was absolutely the right course of action to take for my clients.

On October 29, 2008, one of Hank's Banks asked Dorothy and my other clients for help in the way of an investment of private capital. On November 14, we invested $14 million. In a small way, I guess you could say, my clients participated in their own private investment to help one of the most powerful financial giants in the world, and they were rewarded for their commitment. Yes, Dorothy, free markets do exist in both fearful and abundant times.

DOING THE RIGHT THING

For a few weeks in October 2008, it was terrifying to see the events on Wall Street. We were undergoing a financial Armageddon, and the effects would inevitably spill over into the rest of the world. I was not alone in expecting the worst; many professionals in the field—savvy, experienced investors who were truly in the know— understood how close we were to losing everything.

At the time of our opportunity, many of Hank's Banks were facing losses on toxic assets. Perhaps without the investment of the free markets and our government, more banks may have faced the same fate as Lehman Brothers and would have disappeared from the financial landscape of the investment universe.

Our investment of $14 million in private funding in the bank would prove itself fruitful within three months' time. By February of 2009, the bank had made significant gains in restructuring itself and its debt. The investment that they had agreed to just three short months earlier looked to be expensive now, and they wished to unwind my note. That was when they came back to me.

I had inserted a three-year call to prevent this very thing from happening. Thus, when they approached me to redeem or renegotiate the note—in exchange for which I would undo the three-year call—I had the upper hand at the bargaining table. I played hardball, not because I could, but because I had to look out for my clients' interests. The bank and I had struck a deal at an hour when the bank needed our help most. Now that the threat of imminent collapse had receded, they wanted out of our deal. But doing that would cost them.

I agreed to unwind half of the $14 million and restructured the note so that my clients would continue to earn a very favorable rate set at 13.5 percent for twenty-four months. The original half of the senior note remained intact at 10.75 percent. The new note was slightly different in structure and carried with it a different type of risk that warranted a higher return.

Again the bank came back to me another year later, and this time, we created a 10 percent one-year note.

The net result was this: during a time when many Americans lost a quarter of their investments, my clients saw a triple digit cumulative return on their invested capital over four years and three months and a safe return of *all* their original investment in Hank's Banks. In addition, because we delivered the profits to my clients as capital gains, they paid a much lower rate of tax on their profits.

I had done the right thing. By remaining flexible within a crisis, while adhering to the broad overall parameters of my efficient portfolio model, I felt I had helped in a small way to protect Dorothy's portfolio, and the portfolios of my other clients, during one of the worst financial meltdowns in history.

FLEXIBILITY BASICS

Black Swan Events are unpredictable by their very nature. When such an event occurs, as it did in September and October 2008, the only path to survival is to remain flexible and to sometimes engage in outside-the-box thinking. Flexibility enabled me to take advantage of the unique opportunity one of Hank's Banks presented to me and, as a result, my clients benefited.

It would be nice if we could assume that no more Black Swan

Events await us in the near future of our financial markets. Unfortunately, given the state of affairs in today's markets—including conditions such as integrated, high-speed stock trading, the continued creation of derivatives and other highly speculative and highly leveraged instruments, and the general lack of morality on Wall Street—the unexpected can probably be expected more and more frequently. The "Flash Crash" of May 6, 2010, when the Dow dropped a thousand points, only to recover them within minutes; the collapse of Knight Capital, a major market-maker on the New York Stock Exchange, due to a software glitch; the illegal fixing of the LIBOR rate, a key benchmark interest rate for European banks: these dramatic and debilitating events are just the tip of the same iceberg that almost sank the world's financial system in the fall of 2008. Each of these events developed unseen, away from the public eye and the attention of the financial press. But each of them affected thousands of investors and millions of dollars. As long as the unexpected can occur, investors—and especially their advisors—must remain flexible, poised, and able to take action when action is called for.

Not only can the economy and financial markets produce Black Swan Events, but such events can also occur on an individual basis. A sudden health emergency, a divorce (either that of a client or of the adult child of a client who suddenly becomes more dependent on the client for support), a corporate downsizing, a serious accident, a lawsuit that goes the wrong way: events like these can have a devastating and utterly unexpected effect on your finances. In the face of such changes, flexibility is key on your part and on the part of your financial advisors.

Following are some key questions you should consider as you think about how you can stay flexible and able to respond to unexpected or unpredictable market or personal developments.

How can you keep up with a changing market? The financial markets are a complex network of large corporations, financial professionals, advisors, government agencies, and scores of other players, each of them with a unique agenda and varying degrees of influence. To put it simply, it can be a confusing place. As an independent investor, what should you be watching to stay abreast of market developments?

This is another place where good communication with your financial advisor is a big plus. For example, in my wealth advising practice, we are in constant communication with clients via media alerts, media webcasts, e-mail, and e-newsletters informing them of current issues that affect the markets. I frequently appear on financial media shows to talk about the economy and financial markets. We frequently host quarterly webinars for my clients and their families and interested friends to discuss current issues and strategies for keeping and building wealth, as well as techniques for passing that wealth to the next generation efficiently. We also provide private wealth investment presentations. Educating via the media has proven itself to be a valuable tool in times of crisis. For example, during the 2008 market crash, we sponsored regular and frequent webinars with my colleagues and with experts from Dimensional Fund Advisors in order to educate and inform my clients about the crisis. Understanding how markets work—and why—in fearful and abundant times only serves to reiterate the message of how we are rewarded for the risk taken in globally diverse capital markets.

The bottom line is this: I want my clients to be well informed and aware of how their portfolio design will aid them in avoiding many of the pitfalls the market can create. Any good financial advisor will wish the same and will work to provide a filter between you and the proponents of the greed/fear cycle, allowing only information with a rational basis through.

How do you know when to take action? As we've already seen, markets can react with stunning swiftness to a precipitating event. Economic news, a financial scandal, a terrorist act, the outbreak of war—any one of these might set off market gyrations that can unnerve even the most seasoned investors. Sometimes these gyrations prove to be only temporary aberrations, and the market reasserts itself in a more stable pattern in a relatively short time. At other times, such fluctuations might indicate a long-term fundamental change in the market that has far-reaching implications for the financial world as a whole.

How do you know which is which? How can you tell whether the market is sending out mayday signals or whether it's only doing temporary acrobatics? Answer: you cannot time the market! Thus the best offense is a great defense. Your overall asset allocation and the diversification of your portfolio, assuming these are correlated to your risk tolerance, should smooth the short-term bumps in the road to long-term capital appreciation and wealth accumulation.

Once again, this is where an experienced wealth advisor can make your life so much easier. My clients know that I am available to work through market scenarios with them, counseling them on the best strategies for their goals. During the October 2008 meltdown, my clients didn't have to call me; I was reaching out proactively to them in my attempt to create a bridge over the troubled waters of those turbulent days. I believe that each investor should expect his or her financial advisor to have the client's best interest so much at heart that he or she will make only those recommendations that are right for clients, and this is especially true in troubled times.

There are also some good books and websites that I direct clients to. These are sources of solid information that aren't touting the "product of the month" or the latest get-rich-quick market trick. Here are some of my favorites:

- *A Random Walk Down Wall Street* by Burton G. Malkiel (W. W. Norton & Co., revised and updated 2003) does a great job of explaining modern portfolio theory and market efficiency in a way that the average investor can understand.

- *An Inflation Primer: Prices, Debt, and the Declining Dollar* by Melchior Palyi (Kessinger Publishing, LLC, 2010 reprint of 1961 original publication) is a classic reference on the impact of inflation, and is as current today as when it was written. I use it extensively to help my clients understand the importance of building protection against inflation into their portfolios.

- *360 Degrees of Financial Literacy* (www.360financialliteracy. org), a website sponsored by the American Institute of Certified Public Accountants (AICPA), has practical information on everything from taxes to estate planning. They also host live webinars on topics of current interest.

- For investment information, Dimensional Fund Advisors (www.dfaus.com). In addition to information about Dimensional and its investment philosophy and strategies, the site contains great research articles on a variety of investment topics.

- *The Investment Answer* by Daniel C. Goldie, CFP, and Gordon S. Murry (Business Plus, 2011). This book does an excellent job of teaching the basics of investing in plain English for both beginning and experienced investors.

- The website for the Financial Industry Regulatory Authority (www.finra.org) is a great place for investors to learn about industry best practices, the basics of finance, and how the markets work.

- Mint.com makes your life easier. Money is for living, so Mint makes everything on its site simple and streamlined, and it takes less than five minutes to get started. Mint pulls all your financial information into one place, so you can finally get your entire net worth delivered to your inbox weekly. I refer to it as "the budget app for people who hate to budget."

- Finally, the Morningstar Inc. website (www.morningstar
.com) offers comprehensive information about mutual
funds and their performance, as well as good general
investing information.

How do you know when to expand on your investment? You may
have heard the saying that in Chinese, the symbol for the word
"crisis" is composed of the symbols for two other words: "dan-
ger" and "opportunity." There is truth in this: almost every crisis
presents opportunities for those who stay calm and aware. As my
experience with one of Hank's Banks in 2008 demonstrated, a crisis in the investment world rewarded my clients. An opportunity
presented itself, and by remaining calm and disciplined, I was able
to capitalize on that opportunity.

Roses Among the Thorns: Launching the Dimensional Fund Advisors' Short-Term Extended Credit Fund

As some of my clients needed a monthly "drip" income from their
portfolios, in November 2008, I switched investments toward more
income-oriented ones. At the time, I was engaged in discussions
with Dimensional Fund Advisors about providing my clients with
fund solutions that addressed that need. I explained the importance of the "drip" to my clients' portfolios, as well as my need
for funds that could generate higher monthly "drip" income.
To my delight, not only did Dimensional have such an idea in
the research lab, but they were open to working with advisors in
order to bring the right solution to market. I worked closely with
Dimensional Fund Advisors and another advisor to develop the
ideas for a short-term corporate bond fund, which Dimensional
then launched on March 6, 2009. The concept was exactly what I
needed to complement my clients' portfolio income needs and

Dimensional proved more than capable of assisting in satisfying those income needs with this new fund.

In January 2009, corporate bonds were perceived as, let's say, less than desirable to hold by the general public. The investing public had become disenchanted with rating agencies like Moody's and S&P because they were intertwined with the subprime mortgage bonds debacle, and their failure to correctly diagnose and grade the toxic assets was a contributing factor to the stock market decline of October 2008. Investors had opted out of lending to companies because they no longer had faith in the integrity of the rating agencies, and thus they no longer trusted their ratings of corporate debt securities. The rating agencies had lost their credibility.

However, bond ratings were not the only criterion in making a fixed investment decision. Dimensional believes in a market-driven approach to "add value" for advisors and their clients. This solution would prove no different, with three elements that distinguish it from other funds:

- Varying allocation between government and credits
- Varying allocation within the credit range (upper and lower tiers)
- Applying variable maturity in government and credit allocations

Accordingly, we created a no-load mutual fund that emphasizes maximum total return by providing the flexibility to invest in a full range of investment grade bonds, extending into the universe of US and foreign corporate debt securities as well as US Treasury Securities. Because corporate debt was not popular at the time and because prices were depressed, it proved to be a very fortuitous time to launch the fund, although I attribute this to my desire to solve the needs of my clients' portfolios and nothing more.

Confident that free markets would return again at some point and that capitalism would once again prevail, the Short-Term Extended Quality Portfolio (DFEQX) was born. As an advocate for my clients, the driving force behind the creation of the fund was to secure a very liquid, short-term vehicle that would pay a solid stream of monthly income and fill the need of credit diversification for my clients.

Beyond the consultative process with Dimensional, my firm along with the other advisor involved in the development of the fund actually committed assets at the launch of the fund on March 6, 2009, priced at $10 a share. When launched, I thought to myself that the fund would provide the income. Secretly I was hoping that in two years we might see a total return in the double digits, but this was my personal desire.

By the end of 2009, after factoring in the monthly dividend payout and the appreciation in the bond fund, my clients had experienced that "personal desire" for a total return in half the time I'd once thought. Against the backdrop of an over 30 percent decline in the Dow Jones Index and a 60 percent fall in international markets, Dimensional's Short-Term Extended Quality Portfolio posted double digit returns. Altogether, it was a very impressive performance.

Sometimes, a market dip can be a major opportunity. But how do you know which dips represent the opportunities? Remember the Wall Street adage: if everybody knows it, it's either wrong or too late. Another way I sometimes say this to my clients is, "If you wait, it's too late." Thus being fully invested in the global markets in conjunction with a written investment plan will build in the flexibility to act. When working with a solid asset allocation and ultra-diverse investment plan, there's no need to be afraid of purchasing in a down market. As long your investment allocation (e.g. 40 percent stock/60 percent fixed income) is commensurate with your ability to stay in the market for the long term, you can view downturns in the markets as opportunities to purchase 10 or 20 percent more investment for your cash. This flexibility doesn't represent timing the market or acting on hunches; rather, it is implementing the goal of creating *wealth by design.*

STAY DIVERSIFIED, STAY THE COURSE

As I said previously, it would be wonderful if you could know that there were no more meteors hurtling through space on a collision course with the financial markets. But no one can give you that assurance. Uncertainty is a fact of life, and the only alternative to constant anxiety or hiding under a rock—neither is very appealing—is to be prepared. You must position yourself to weather that storm, whenever it comes, in whatever form it takes.

Remember: level heads prevail, and luck favors the prepared. Block out the noise created by the media; disregard the investment pornography. It might surprise you to hear me say this, but I actually discourage my clients to some degree from reading financial publications or watching the financial shows on television. If they are viewing the financial media, I teach them to filter out what's useful and educational from what is mere entertainment or investment pornography.

Why? Isn't an educated investor a smart investor? Yes, but the media will rarely make you an educated investor. What it will make you is impulsive, speculative, and prone to succumbing to the greed/fear cycle I described in chapter four.

Instead, trust in your portfolio design and keep to your plan.

If you are maintaining a balanced asset allocation for your risk profile and adequately diversifying within your asset classes, you will be able to ride out future investment storms. And being ultra-diversified globally will help to minimize the downside damage to your overall portfolio while not requiring your money to work as hard on the upside. By focusing on your overall investment strategy and portfolio and by taking a big-picture approach with your advisor or on your own, you will avoid undisciplined, seat-of-the-pants portfolio turnovers that get the majority of investors in trouble.

As we've established, risk is *not* best evaluated on an asset-by-asset basis. Instead, each investment should be evaluated as to its singular contribution to the portfolio's total return. This broad focus is possible when your portfolio is appropriately diversified. Diversification is your best defense against any down market, especially in today's volatile financial landscape—and especially concerning the equity portion of your investments.

The graphic on the following page illustrates a fully diversified portfolio for a client who holds 40 percent of his assets in fixed income investments and 60 percent in equities.

ALWAYS IN THE MARKET

Just to make sure I'm perfectly clear on this point: I am opposed to emotion-driven, reactive attempts to time the market that cause people to liquidate their holdings on the advice of fear-mongers. My clients were invested in the markets in 2008, 2009, 2010, and all the days since. By exercising discipline and designing portfolios that follow sound, proven principles, my clients are not subjected to jumping in and out of investments in a self-defeating way.

We are able to stay invested because we follow a plan that has been proven to work, no matter what type of market we are experiencing at the moment. I keep my clients in the market because

A Hypothetical Fully Diversified Portfolio

MODEL PORTFOLIO 5

Components

Legend:
- One-Year US Treasury Note Index
- S&P 500 Index
- US Small Cap Index
- US Large Value Index
- Targeted Value Index
- International Large Index
- International Small Index
- International Large Value Index
- International Small Value Index
- Emerging Markets Blended Index

Key Characteristics

	Hypothetical Annualized Compound Return	Hypothetical Annualized Standard Deviation
Model Portfolio 1	9.34%	11.14%
Model Portfolio 2	8.65%	10.27%
Model Portfolio 3	9.46%	11.95%
Model Portfolio 4	10.33%	11.94%
Model Portfolio 5	11.15%	11.39%

Percentages

	Govt./Credit Bond Index	S&P 500 Index	One-Year US Treasury Note Index	US Small Cap Index	US Large Value Index	Targeted Value Index	Intl. Large Index	Intl. Small Index	Intl. Large Value Index	Intl. Small Value Index	Emerging Markets Blended Index
Model Portfolio 1	40%	60%									
Model Portfolio 2		60%	40%								
Model Portfolio 3		30%	40%	30%							
Model Portfolio 4		15%	40%	15%	15%	15%					
Model Portfolio 5	7.5%	7.5%	40%	7.5%	7.5%	7.5%	6%	6%	6%	6%	6%

I match their asset allocation mix to their risk tolerance level and I keep them broadly diversified. These solid fundamentals allow us to remain flexible enough to adapt to the rapidly changing circumstances brought about by the market meltdown. Flexibility enabled us to take advantage of the unique opportunities afforded by Hank's Banks and their need for funds and by the very attractive pricing of investment-grade, short-term corporate debt that made up the Dimensional Short-Term Extended Credit Fund.

I can't stress the benefits of a well-conceived and disciplined strategy enough. Some people have the idea that such a focused design is restricting or that it causes you to miss opportunities that less-structured investors might capture. But it really works in the opposite way: when you are following a plan, you aren't being distracted by the "noise" that so easily sidetracks other investors. That means you can actually pay closer attention to the real opportunities—the ones supported by careful research and sound investment principles. Disciplined investors stay invested, stay the course, and reap the benefits; undisciplined investors jump in and out of investments in a vain attempt to capture the latest hot stock or value play, and they invariably achieve inferior returns. The research backs this up, time and time again. That's why I tell my clients: "Stay diversified, and stay the course."

LOOKING AHEAD

I am often asked, "What do you see for the future of the markets?" My response is, "In 2008, my crystal ball shattered, and my new one has been on backorder since."

In short: trying to predict the future is a form of short-term speculation as opposed to "investing," which is long-term wealth accumulation.

The approach to investing that all investors should at least be aware of wasn't developed by the big banks and brokerage firms on Wall Street. It originated and evolved in the halls of academia, and it is based on a mountain of evidence showing that free markets work because the price system is a powerful mechanism for communicating information. As F. A. Hayek pointed out in his 1974 Nobel lecture, "We are only beginning to understand how subtle and efficient the communication mechanism we call the market is. It garners, comprehends, and disseminates widely dispersed information better and faster than any system man has deliberately designed."[7]

So what does this mean to you as an investor? Simply that stock prices are fair. Competition among profit-seeking investors causes prices to change very quickly in response to new information, and neither the buyer nor the seller of a publicly traded security has a systematic advantage. Therefore, the current price is our best estimate of fair value.

Despite the strength of market forces, many investors (and sometimes even my clients) succumb to eliciting an opinion about the market from me and other professionals. And on these occasions, I do offer my outlook for the future. I am reminded of what a mentor of mine once told me: "I am happy to share with you my opinion of the future, but I don't make investment decisions based on opinion—yours or anyone else's." If the compulsion to act on an opinion is too difficult for your investors to resist, ask them if it is conceivable that they are the only ones with the information upon which their opinion is based. If the answer is no and the information is widely known, then why wouldn't it already be reflected in prices? For example, the claim that "everyone knows interest rates

_____

7. The full text is available online at www.nobelprize.org/nobel_prizes /economics/laureates/1974/hayek-lecture.html.

are going up" should be met with the fundamental premise that if the statement were literally true, rates would have already gone up! The logic behind how markets work is a formidable response to any forecast of the future.

The prediction business is also complicated by the continual possibility—in fact, likelihood—of Black Swan Events. Indeed, as Taleb points out, no one, as late as the 1980s, projected the value of the Internet, even though the basic principles that make the Internet possible have been in operation for some five decades. No one in the early 1900s anticipated the 1929 stock market crash that helped precipitate the Great Depression. Because no one can forecast these kinds of determining influences on the market with any certainty or accuracy, my advice is to stop listening to the prophets and prognosticators. But if you really want a glimpse into the future, I'll give you one. Here is my prediction about the future. Are you ready?

The future will happen.

It's as simple as that. I have no theories on what the future will actually be like to live in. I have no ideas about any new discoveries that will change everything. Because I have no such theories— and because I'm wise enough to know I have no such theories—I choose to frame the way I think about the future differently. Rather than view the future as something uncertain to be feared, a place where I have no power to accurately determine major events, I prepare financially for the future by planning for various possible scenarios.

"As one projects into the future, one needs to increase the precision about the process one is modeling, since one's error rate grows so rapidly the further one projects."
—Henri Poincaré, mathematician and philosopher

Because my crystal ball is broken, the following are *talking points*. Rather than being the result of some mystic vision, they are simply sound principles that make sense to me based on my experience as a wealth advisor, as well as on what I see currently developing in the financial and economic landscape.

Debt

One very important key to successfully weathering the uneven waters ahead of us is to pay off all debt, especially high-cost credit card debts and car loans. Pay off variable rate credit cards and personal debt with adjustable rates. If you can manage it, pay off your home mortgage in its entirety. In the 2008 crash, many people lost their homes through foreclosures—don't let that happen to you. If you cannot pay off your mortgage, the next best step is to take advantage of current historically low interest rates and refinance the loan for a fixed thirty-year term at a lower cost to you. If you have an adjustable-rate home equity loan, refinance to a low rate fixed loan, or pay it off as well.

Cash

I think it will be increasingly necessary to have cash reserves on hand. It is a good idea to have at least twelve to eighteen months' worth of emergency funds. Reduce your spending to "live below your means but within your needs," the mantra my clients hear from me religiously. Many of my wealthy clients achieved wealth not through a windfall or inheritance, but by implementing this very mantra.

Commodities

All commodities have had stellar price performances in recent years, this is true. But commodities are not "investments," as they do not generate intrinsic wealth. If you must invest in commodities, invest in a no-load mutual fund designed to seek total return in a portfolio that invests in a universe of commodity-linked derivative instruments and fixed income investments. This assists in providing a hedge against inflation, but also creates current income from short-term fixed income of durations of three years or less. If you wish to buy physical gold, you may purchase it either in gold bars, gold coins, or gold jewelry, but physical gold would be, in the very worst case, a bartering tool for other goods and services. If you have any gold jewelry that you don't regularly wear, sell it. Current gold prices are hovering around record highs due to strong investment demand from China and India, so why not sell it now and stash the cash in your emergency fund?

Equities

Everyone should maintain some exposure to equities—the stock market—to benefit from the strong earnings streams of well-managed companies. However, your optimum degree of exposure depends on your age, your earnings potential, and the financial assets you already have on hand. The younger you are, the longer your investing horizon is and the more risks you can afford to take. The flip side of this is that the younger you are, the more chance inflation has to eat away steadily at the value of your holdings, and historically, the stock market has offered the best opportunities for protection against inflation erosion. Don't forget the importance of asset allocation: how much of your wealth you invest in equities depends on the factors I've mentioned above. (See appendix for sample portfolios.) But to have no money in the stock market is, for most investors, a mistake.

Deep Cuts?

The bulk of investors who experienced the decline in their portfolios during the dotcom bust of the early 2000s and in the most recent crash of 2008 will never fully recover. Why? Simple: the key to successful investing in equities is to understand your risk tolerance. It means knowing how much you can afford to lose and still stay invested in the global markets. Can you survive a repeat of the crash of 2008, or an even greater crash? Or is your equity exposure too high and too volatile for you? Talk to your wealth advisor about this very important point.

Fixed Income

Especially for investors aged sixty and older, I am focusing the fixed-income portion of their portfolios on short-term bonds and notes. By short term, I refer to an average duration of five years or less. (If a portfolio consists of a bond that takes nine years to mature, a second one that matures in five years, and another with a two-year maturity, the average duration of this portfolio will be about five years.)

The financial world is still very unsettled. The strategy behind maintaining short durations in our fixed-income portfolios is to maintain flexibility in these disruptive times as the financial world shifts and shakes to reach equilibrium. By maintaining short durations, I am seeking to decrease interest-rate risk.

Here's an illustration of interest-rate risk. If you were fully invested in a thirty-year bond with a 5 percent coupon, and the Fed increased interest rates from 5 percent to 10 percent, you would be stuck with an underperforming asset because bond prices fall when interest rates rise. Your natural thought may be to sell the bond, but all the other holders of bonds with a 5 percent coupon will also be seeking a quick exit, creating lots of supply and not much demand. After all, when an investor can earn 10 percent on newly issued bonds, why would she want yours, which only pays 5 percent? That means that the only way you can unload your 5 percent bond is to sell it at a steep discount, perhaps as much as 60 percent, which represents a serious hit to your principal.

However, if you have the same interest rate on a one-, two-, or three-year note, you can sell it at a much smaller discount in order to exit—or you can wait for a much shorter time before recovering 100 percent of your principal, which you can then easily reinvest in a bond with a higher coupon.

This illustrates why, in the current environment, I'm focusing on short-term durations. After all, interest rates are at historically low levels; they have just about nowhere to go except up. When that happens, I don't want my fixed-income portfolios to be stuck in long-term bonds.

TIPS

Even fixed-income portfolios need some sort of inflation hedge. For my retired clients, I recommend having 10–15 percent of their fixed-income portfolios invested in Treasury inflation protected securities, also known as TIPS. These are government securities that are tied to inflation such that their par value rises and falls according to the inflation index.

The face value of TIPS is adjusted yearly. For example, let's say you bought a US TIPS bond with a face value of $1,000 and a coupon rate of 2 percent. If inflation goes up by 5 percent that year, in the next year, the face value of the bond will be increased to $1,050 to match the inflation rate. Your interest payments of 2 percent will also increase from $20 to $21, or 2 percent of a bond with a $1,050 face value.

The concept behind TIPS is to protect your purchasing power from being eroded by inflation. If you are retired and fully dependent on a fixed income, this is especially important.

Global, Municipal, and Corporate Bond Funds

Additionally, investors should consider allocating money to a five-year global bond fund to benefit from buoyant economies around the world. Because income from municipal bonds is tax-free, a high-tax-bracket investor should consider a short-term general obligation municipal bond fund. Another option would be a corporate bond fund with A+ ratings or better, or a mutual fund invested in corporate inflation protected securities (IPS).

Inflation: The Silent Thief

The common theme in the fixed-income strategies above is protection against inflation. I'm very focused on this because I believe that inflation is inevitably going to be a problem. Although the good news is that inflation is relatively low now, the bad news is that inflation has only one way to go: up. Without increased inflation, how are we, as a country, going to get rid of our current debt load, which has reached unimaginable proportions?

We are at the crossroads, and there are only two paths ahead of us: to tax our way out of debt, or to inflate our currency to reduce its sting. As it appears that we are no longer able to impose higher tax burdens on the working public, inflation is the logical, default solution.

So . . . brace yourself and prepare for inflation. (Anyone who lived through the double-digit inflation years of the 1970s, when inflation was running at a 15 percent annual rate, will remember that we also had stagflation, the painful combination of high inflation and a stagnant economy. Again, this is a possible outcome.)

Contingent Deferred Annuities:
Portfolio Income Insurance

A concept that I have used with great success for many of my fixed-income portfolios involves combining the use of a contingent deferred annuity (CDA) with other assets to protect clients against the risk of outliving the income stream from their investments. A certain portion of the investment account is designated for coverage by the CDA—in effect, the account is "wrapped"—to guarantee continued income from the assets if inflation pushes the value of the covered assets below the level needed for income.

For illustrative purposes only, let's say that a seventy-year-old investor places investments worth $1 million into the portion of assets covered by a CDA. He immediately begins annual withdrawals of 5 percent of the value of the account, or $50,000, as income. If the value of the assets covered by the CDA falls to zero, the contingent deferred annuity guarantees the payment of $50,000 per year for as long as the investor lives or joint with rights of survivorship. It allows the assets to remain under management with the advisor, ensuring that if unexpected events cause the portfolio to lose its value, a set amount of payments to the client can continue regardless of the value of the portfolio. Essentially, as my mentor once told me nearly twenty years ago, "Investors want the downside protection of a CD, but upside appreciation of the market—that simply doesn't exist." Well, it does exist now, thanks to concepts like the CDA. (For more information, see appendix on CDAs.)

I like to think of this approach as adding a fourth leg to your three-legged retirement stool. The first leg is the Social Security retirement benefit that you've been paying into during your earning years. The second leg could be represented by any pension or retirement plan available to you through your employer or a retirement benefit plan for self-employed persons. The third leg is any other savings that you can use to help fund your retirement lifestyle.

The contingent deferred annuity adds a fourth leg to your stool, providing a guaranteed income stream. So, if one of the other three legs breaks—for example, if Social Security proves less dependable than you had hoped—you've still got three legs left on your stool and you can maintain balance.

Several sophisticated actuarial and financial models exist to help investors determine the optimum asset mix and coverage amounts if they choose to utilize CDAs in their retirement income planning. I have found this "portfolio insurance" idea to be very useful for many of my retiree clients.

Evolving Economy

I believe we are slowly evolving into a one-world, electronically based monetary system and trading system, although how fast this will happen is unknown. Globally, economies are so intertwined with each other that if one suffers financial tsunamis, it is likely to cause ripple effects throughout the remainder of the global markets.

For more evidence of this trend, just look at the continuing concerns over Eurozone sovereign debt, a crisis that started with Greece and spilled over to Portugal and most recently to Ireland and Spain. Although tensions have eased somewhat, there remain residual worries that a continued Eurozone problem will hamstring the global recovery. All of these forces plus overwhelming debt at all levels are moving us inextricably and inevitably toward a changing financial order. Unsettling times will always demand informed flexibility.

And so I'll end this chapter as I began: be flexible. Design a sound plan, work systematically toward your goals, and don't be panicked by financial hearsay—but stay light on your feet. Your financial advisor can help you survive and thrive as long as you follow these basic steps.

STEP 1: DISCOVERING AND SETTING YOUR GOALS

- **What are my needs?** (family obligations, debt commitments, lifestyle requirements)
- **What are my desires?** (difference between a need and a desire)

- **Where do I want to go?** (life goals and relationship to financial goals; short-, mid-, and long-term goals)
- **When is it time to review or revise my goals?**

STEP 2: PLANNING YOUR INVESTMENTS

- **Do I know the fundamentals of investing?**
- **What does my asset allocation currently look like?**
- **What does diversification mean?**
- **Why shouldn't I try to time the market?**
- **What kinds of risk can I tolerate?**

STEP 3: COMMITTING TO YOUR PLAN

- **How do I enact my plan?**
- **How do I commit to that plan?**
- **What problems might challenge my commitment?**

STEP 4: ASSESSING YOUR PLAN

- **What indicators do I look at to determine how well my plan is working?**
- **Is my asset allocation properly balanced?**
- **What's next on my wealth agenda?**

STEP 5: KEEPING YOUR PLAN FLEXIBLE

- **How can I keep up with a changing market?**
- **How do I know when to take action?**
- **How do I know when to expand on my investment?**

THE HIGHEST REWARD

EACH YEAR I send my clients a survey asking for their feedback on how I'm doing as their wealth advisor. Not long ago, I received the results of my most recent survey, and my clients awarded me five out of a possible five points for the categories "Trust in Advisor" and "Demonstrated Leadership in Turbulent Times."

Needless to say, I am deeply proud of the confidence my clients place in me. But I don't think I've done anything out of the ordinary to win that trust. I feel I have done my job. I pay close attention to my clients' goals and strive each day to be guided by the simple principle of doing the right thing. Everything my clients and I have accomplished together—from investing in one of the world's largest banks to participating in the development of the short-term corporate bond fund in response to investors' needs—has been built on the foundation of these simple and—to me, at least—obvious ideas.

But apparently they weren't obvious to everybody. In deciding to take advantage of the Hank's Banks opportunity, I am sure there were critics and maybe even colleagues that thought what I was doing was utterly implausible and foolhardy. As I reflect back on those tumultuous times, I am reminded of a key element of advice that Dan, a mentor of mine, once told me: "Kimberly, always do the right thing for your clients. It may be that the best road for them is the road less traveled, but that is exactly why you are their advisor: to do what is best for their needs. And sometimes that may involve thinking outside the box." Thus when the opportunity presented itself to create the senior debt, I knew it was the right thing to do—and thank you, Dan, for those words of wisdom.

It would take several months before the anxiety over being in a market under such extreme conditions shrank enough for me to sleep through the night. Nevertheless, I trusted in the strength of my investment strategy and the careful design that had gone into my clients' portfolios. It would take a year before my clients fully realized what I had done for them, but they knew from day one that what I was recommending was based on my familiarity with their goals, my knowledge of market conditions, and my bone-deep conviction that this was the best course for them to follow. And in the bargain, we also played a role in preserving the free and orderly financial markets that all of us depend on.

BORN TO PROTECT

It is clear to me now that I was born to protect. Growing up in a big family with financially challenged parents made a huge impact on me. It is without question the reason I entered the financial services industry. From an early age, I sensed a responsibility to financially guard my family. I wanted to take care of my parents and make their lives easier. Perhaps if my parents had been free from worry about money, they could have lived their lives in peace without the teeth of anxiety about money gnawing at their financial security with every paycheck they earned.

That experience also created in me a desire to educate others about money as a tool. If I can guide my clients to make smart financial decisions, their money can work for them as efficiently as possible, giving them more freedom of choice. An educator instinctively leans toward the student to probe and to encourage questions. They ask questions to understand the thinking process, surmise gaps in students' knowledge, and seek the most effective lines of communication, so all will understand.

Similarly, the advisor is always aware and looking for the best information to help clients and investors alike make better, smarter decisions. I strive to be the person others turn to for answers to financial issues. To be useful, of course, my advice always has to be shaped around the unique needs of the individual client.

Ultimately, my work is focused on advancing the greatest good for the greatest number. I thrive in my role as protector, teacher, and advisor, and every decision I've made in my business life has been run through this filter: "Is this in the best interest of my clients?" Nothing else matters.

LEADING WITH INTEGRITY

I believe that integrity is central to leadership. People trust those who lead them, and in my opinion, the leader's underlying principle is to be the protector. We all know it happens in all professions, but it stabs at my heart to see some individuals in leadership roles taking advantage of their position rather than putting the needs of their clients ahead of their own personal agenda. The most important bit of wisdom given to me by my manager at Merrill Lynch was this: "Kimberly, never lose your passion, your integrity, and your gift of leadership. It's the key to your success." He was absolutely correct; I am passionate, and at every turn of advising, I lead with integrity in caring for my clients' financial welfare. And I have no doubt that any success I've achieved or will achieve is predicated on that central passion.

FREE MARKETS, FREEDOM TO DREAM

Like my clients, I believe in free markets. That's where wealth is created. The engine of wealth is propelled by what happens when a need exists and when someone creates a product or service to fill that need. That moment of meeting between need and product is the most decisive event in our American culture. That process, repeated millions of times every day, is what has made us wealthy as a nation and what has given us one of the highest standards of living on the planet.

But that process is also fraught with risk. The reason the wealthy are wealthy is because they're willing to accept that risk. Remember that one of the basic principles throughout this whole book is the relationship between risk and reward. When you invest in the global markets, you must be well prepared. You must remember that asset allocation strategy determines the success of your portfolio and your ability to accumulate wealth over time. You must also remember that diversification is your friend. And when you choose a wealth advisor, make sure you choose one who has your best interest—not his or her next sales commission—at heart.

In the world of financial advisors, I sometimes feel like the exception to the rule. Not all of us see ourselves as wealth advisors or as financial guardians. Not all of us attend clients' family weddings and children's graduations. Not all of us throw a yearly appreciation party for our clients. Not all of us think of our clients as family. I have been told many times by my peers in the industry that I shouldn't take my clients' interests and portfolios so much to heart.

But I can't do business any other way. And it is my belief that my clients deserve a wealth advisor who is passionate about serving their needs and helping them meet their goals.

It is true that there are many random events in the financial marketplace. But your approach to building your wealth cannot be random. It must be carefully considered, meticulously planned, backed by solid commitments, and regularly assessed. When these steps are followed—and when you and your advisor can maintain flexibility in challenging times—you will have put in place the strategy that will empower you to meet your goals and live your dreams. You will achieve wealth, but not as the result of random events, lucky breaks, or "timing the market." Instead, you will become Wealthy by Design.

ACKNOWLEDGMENTS

FIRST, I WOULD like to thank you, the reader, for investing in this book. As I stated in the final chapter of this book, you will not achieve wealth as a result of random events, lucky breaks, or "timing the market." Instead, my hope is that you will implement the steps outlined within this book so that you may become *Wealthy by Design*.

Over the years, I have learned much from my clients, whom I am fortunate to work with every day. Thank you for trusting me to offer guidance and to work in your best interests. A special thanks to the clients who enthusiastically offered their individual stories in the hopes of helping others with similar investment challenges.

Thank you to my staff, especially Joanne Nuguit, Director of Client Affairs; Renee Morrison, Comptroller; and Lynda Burkett, Operations Manager, of Empyrion Wealth Management, Inc. Throughout this project, you kept the office running smoothly. I very much appreciate your hard work and dedication to our clients.

Thank you to my expert team at Greenleaf Book Group: the CEO, Clint Greenleaf; my main contacts, Justin Branch and Natalie Navar; my editor, Lari Bishop; designer Kim Lance; distribution guru Angela Alwin; and everybody else who has helped take this project from idea to market.

To my friends and colleagues at Dimensional Fund Advisors: I've been fortunate to be an advisor since 1993, and Dimensional's investment philosophy has created a paradigm shift in my practice, and in turn, created overall wealth for my clients. A big thank you to Bill Wiggins, my trusted bond specialist; you have an amazing tenacity for the bond market, and your level of integrity in "the business" is second to no one!

Finally, thank you to my family: my amazing husband, Charles; my daughter, Madison; my stepdaughter, Sara; my stepson, Christopher; and my youngest angel, Jack Ryan. We are blessed to have an amazing family and I look forward to our next big adventure together. I love you all, especially you, my one true love, Charles.

QUESTIONS TO ASK A PROSPECTIVE FINANCIAL ADVISOR

THE FOLLOWING ARE some example questions you can (and should) use when seeking a financial advisor:

1. Do you have experience in providing advice on the topics below? If yes, indicate the number of years.
   - Retirement planning
   - Investment planning
   - Tax planning
   - Estate planning
   - Insurance planning
   - Integrated planning
   - Other

2. What are your areas of specialization?
   What qualifies you in this field?

3. a. How long have you been offering financial planning advice to clients?

- Less than one year
- One to four years
- Five to ten years
- More than ten years

b. How many clients do you usually have?

- Less than 10
- 10 to 39
- 40 to 79
- 80+

4. Briefly describe your work history.

5. What are your educational qualifications? Give any areas of study.

- Certificate
- Undergraduate degree
- Advanced degree
- Other

6. What financial planning designation(s) or certification(s) do you hold?

- Certified Financial Planner (CFP)
- Certified Public Accountant–Personal Financial Specialist (CPA–PFS)
- Chartered Financial Consultant (ChFC)
- Other

7. What financial planning continuing education requirements do you fulfill?

8. What licenses do you hold?

- Insurance
- Securities
- CPA
- J.D.
- Other

9. a. Are you personally licensed or registered as an investment advisor representative with a state?

- Yes
- No
  If no, why not?

b. Are you or your firm licensed or registered as an investment advisor with the

- State?
- Federal government?
  If neither, why not?

c. Will you provide me with your disclosure document Form ADV Part II or its state equivalent?

- Yes
- No
  If no, why not?

10. What services do you offer?

11. Describe your approach to financial planning.

12. a. Who will work with me?

- Planner
- Associate(s)

b. Will the same individual(s) review my financial situation?

- Yes
- No
  If no, who will?

13. How are you paid for your services?

- Fee
- Commission
- Fee and commission
- Salary
- Other

14. What do you typically charge?

a. Fee:

- Hourly rate: $____
- Flat fee (range): $____ to $____
- Percentage of assets under management: ____ percent

b. Commission:

What is the approximate percentage of the investment or premium you receive on:

- stocks and bonds: ____ percent
- mutual funds: ____ percent
- annuities: ____ percent
- insurance products: ____ percent
- other: ____ percent

15. a. Do you have a business affiliation with any company whose products or services you are recommending?

- Yes
- No

Explain:

b. Is any of your compensation based on selling products?

- Yes
- No
  Explain:

c. Do professionals and sales agents to whom you may refer me send business, fees, or any other benefits to you?

- Yes
- No
  Explain:

d. Do you have an affiliation with a broker/dealer?

- Yes
- No
  Explain:

e. Are you an owner of, or connected with, any other company whose services or products I use?

- Yes
- No
  Explain:

16. Do you provide a written client engagement agreement?

- Yes
- No
  If no, why not?

SIX PORTFOLIO ALLOCATION STRATEGIES

THE GRAPHIC ON the following page shows six possible strategies for allocating your portfolio along different ratios of equity to fixed income, and is included courtesy of Dimensional Fund Advisors.

Sample Allocations

	FIXED	CONSERVATIVE	MODERATE	NORMAL	AGGRESSIVE	EQUITY
EQUITY	**0.0%**	**20.0%**	**40.0%**	**60.0%**	**80.0%**	**100.0%**
US STOCKS	**0.0%**	**14.0%**	**28.0%**	**42.0%**	**56.0%**	**70.0%**
LARGE CAP	0.0	4.0	8.0	12.0	16.0	20.0
LARGE CAP VALUE	0.0	4.0	8.0	12.0	16.0	20.0
SMALL CAP	0.0	2.0	4.0	6.0	8.0	10.0
SMALL CAP VALUE	0.0	2.0	4.0	6.0	8.0	10.0
REAL ESTATE STRATEGY	0.0	2.0	4.0	6.0	8.0	10.0
NON-US STOCKS	**0.0%**	**6.0%**	**12.0%**	**18.0%**	**24.0%**	**30.0%**
VALUE	0.0	2.0	4.0	6.0	8.0	10.0
SMALL CAP	0.0	1.0	2.0	3.0	4.0	5.0
SMALL CAP VALUE	0.0	1.0	2.0	3.0	4.0	5.0
EMERGING MARKETS	0.0	0.6	1.2	1.8	2.4	3.0
EMERGING MARKETS VALUE	0.0	0.6	1.2	1.8	2.4	3.0
EMERGING MARKETS SMALL CAP	0.0	0.8	1.6	2.4	3.2	4.0
FIXED INCOME	**100.0%**	**80.0%**	**60.0%**	**40.0%**	**20.0%**	**0.0%**
ONE-YEAR	25.0	20.0	15.0	10.0	5.0	0.0
TWO-YEAR GLOBAL	25.0	20.0	15.0	10.0	5.0	0.0
FIVE-YEAR GOVERNMENT	25.0	20.0	15.0	10.0	5.0	0.0
FIVE-YEAR GLOBAL	25.0	20.0	15.0	10.0	5.0	0.0

INDEX

A

AIG, 119

allocation. See asset allocation

American Institute of Certified Public Accountants (AICPA), 139

America, opportunities in, 39, 42–43

annuities, 62–63, 153–55

assessing your plan, 95–113
    asset allocation, 105–7
    indicators for, 105
    need for, 95–96
    overview, 95, 113
    rebalancing, 105–7
    sixty-day follow-up, 4–5, 98–99, 105

assessments, 26–28, 92

asset allocation
    and diversification, 54, 142–44
    matching to risk tolerance, 69–71, 96, 146
    overview, 54–57
    portfolio allocation strategies, 169–70
    and purchasing in down market, 142–43
    and rebalancing, 105–7
    See also diversification

assets under management (AUM), 23, 83

Auburn, California, 11

B

Bank of America, 121

banks
    bolstering reserves, 41
    CD interest rates, 40–41
    hoarding cash, 3
    investment banks' conversion to commercial, 122–24
    leveraging regulations, 121–22
    and real estate bubble, 40
    Texas Premium CDs, 41
    See also CDs; "Hank's Banks"

Barclays PLC, 117

Bear Stearns, 117

Berkshire Hathaway, 56, 123

Birr Wilson, 49–51

Black Swan Events
    diversification and allocation as buffer, 142–44
    individual, 136
    market, 135–36
    opportunity within, 140–42
    overview, 115–16, 135
    See also October 10, 2008, DJIA plunge

bond indexes, 59

bonds
    bond funds, 152–53
    diversification in, 58–59
    for fixed-income investors, 50, 151–52
    interest from, 62
    interest-rate risk, 59, 70, 151–52
    maturity date diversification, 59
    Short-Term Extended Quality Portfolio, 140–42

breaking the buck, 117–18

Brinson, Hood, and Beebower, 54

Buffett, Warren, 56, 122–23

C

California State University, Chico (CSUC), 45–48

call option on CDs, 127–28

case studies
    Gen Xer, spender, 19–21, 91, 108
    retirees, 31–33

'tweeners, 65–67
   See also Dorothy
cash-equivalent class, 62
cash reserves, 149
CDAs (contingent deferred annuities),
   62–63, 153–55
CDs
   interest rates, 40–41, 69
   one-year call options, 127–28
   as steady income investment, 62
challenges and obstacles, addressing,
   91–92
client/financial advisor relationship
   client correspondence, 97–99
   client enjoys playing the market,
      64–65
   communication and attention,
      30–31
   feedback surveys, 157
   keeping clients informed, 137,
      143–44
   reaching out during trouble times,
      138
   responding to client questions, 50
clients
   debts/financial obligations, 27,
      149
   enjoys playing the market, 64–65
   types of, 6
commission-based financial advisor
   active portfolio management, 53,
      96, 97, 99
   fee-based vs., 83, 84, 87, 102, 104
commitment to your plan, 73–93
   author opens her own company,
      82–84
   author's plan to work for Merrill
      Lynch, 74–79
   author's success at Merrill Lynch,
      80–82
   challenges to your commitment,
      91–92
   client/financial advisor
      commitment meeting, 85,
      88–92
   enacting the plan, 89–90
   mechanics of, 90–91
   overview, 4–5, 73, 84–85, 93
commodities, 149–50

communication
   client correspondence, 97–99
   client/financial advisor
      commitment meeting, 85,
      88–92
   individualized e-mails, 131
   as priority in client/financial
      advisor relationship, 86
   responding to client questions, 50
   well-informed clients as result of,
      137, 143–44
   See also assessing your plan
consultative advisor. See fee-based
   financial advisor
contingent deferred annuities (CDAs),
   62–63, 153–55
corporate bond funds, 152–53
credit freeze, 120
credit markets and toxic assets, 1, 3,
   40, 116
crises. See Black Swan Events
Current Income Estimate Report, 24

D
death put option, 127
debt load of United States, 153
debts/financial obligations, 27, 149
desires. See dreams and desires
Dimensional Fund Advisors
   investment tools, 110–12, 139
   mutual funds, 23–24, 98, 109–12,
      140–42
   overview, 109–10
   Short-Term Extended Quality
      Portfolio, 140–42
discovery principle, 4–5. See also
   goals
diversification
   allocation and, 54, 142–44
   as buffer in difficult market,
      143–44
   in equities, 60–61
   overview, 53, 57–60
   portfolio example, 145
   and rebalancing, 106–7
   See also asset allocation
dividends
   from equities, 62

as steady income, 50, 56
See also bonds
Dominican University, 34–35
Dorothy (women in transition case study)
    allocation chart, 68
    commitment meeting, 88–89
    goals of, 29, 67, 69
    and "Hank's Bank" financial product, 132–34
    investment plan considerations, 91
Dow Jones (DJIA), 30–31. See also equities; October 10, 2008, DJIA plunge; stock market
dreams and desires
    assessing, 28
    client enjoys playing the market, 64–65
    financial freedom, 25–31
    free market as enabler, 160–61
    power of, 10–11
    wealth agenda, 107–8
    See also goals
"drip" philosophy, 50, 62–63, 140–42

E

efficient portfolios, 52, 109–10
elementary-grade teacher, 35–36
emotions
    and decision making, 22–23, 101
    greed/fear cycle, 99–101, 102, 104
Enron, 57
equities
    diversification in, 60–61
    dividends from, 62
    as hedge against inflation, 55, 56
    maintaining exposure to, 150
    risks associated with, 56–57, 150–51
    See also stock market
Eurozone, 155
events affecting needs, 27–28, 31. See also Black Swan Events
evolving economy, 155

F

family background, 18–19, 47, 79
fear/greed cycle, 99–101, 102, 104
Federal Reserve, 3, 119, 121, 122
fee-based financial advisor
    author's decision for, 83–84
    commission-based firms vs., 83, 84, 87, 102, 104
    overview, 23
    value-add portfolio management, 53, 96, 97, 99
feedback surveys from clients, 157
financial advisor
    characteristics of, 49, 50–51, 159
    childhood of, 9–10
    choosing your, 43–44, 86–87
    need for, 21–23
    and principles for financial security, 4–5
    questions for, before hiring, 5, 23, 25, 163–67
    See also commission-based financial advisor; fee-based financial advisor
financial freedom, goals for achieving, 25–31
Financial Industry Regulatory Authority (FINRA), 139
financial media shows, 137
financial product for "Hank's Bank," 125, 126–29
fixed income ("drip"), 50, 62–63, 140–42
fixed-income investors, 50, 151–52. See also Dorothy
Flash Crash, May 6, 2010, 136
flexibility, 115–56
    and asset allocation, 142–43
    communication as cornerstone, 136–37
    and diversification, 143–44
    and expanding your investment, 140, 142–43
    and market variability, 137–40
    need for, 135–36
    overview, 4–5, 156
    and staying in the market, 144, 146

and well-informed clients, 137,
    143–44
  See also investment planning
Fooled by Randomness (Taleb),
    115–16
Foss, Kimberly
  ancestors, 11–15
  childhood, 14–15, 16–17, 46
  college years, 45–48
  feedback from clients, 157
  financial planning career choice,
    47–48, 158–59
  "Hank's Bank" investment
    structure, 125–29
  integrity of, 43, 83, 159–61
  Jordache jeans for, 15–16
  and Merrill Lynch, 48, 74–78,
    80–82
  and October 10, 2008, DJIA
    plunge, 3–4, 33–34, 119–21
  personal finance and brokerage
    experience, 49–51
  Series 7 Licensing Examination,
    78–79
  starting Erickson & Associates,
    82–84
Franklin Planner for time
    management, 78–79
free market system, 147–48, 160–61
future, predicting the, 102, 146–49
future talking points, 149–55

G

Gates, Bill, 56
genetics and financial tendencies, 19
Gen Xers and Yers, 6, 56
global bond funds, 152
global economy, 3, 59, 155
goals, 9–37
  author's while growing up, 15–17
  couples defining mutual goals, 32
  as discovery aspect of financial
    planning, 4–5
  Dominican University study,
    34–35
  of elementary student, 35–36

importance of, 18–19, 25–31
  initial direction, 25–26
  integrating investment plan,
    65–69
  needs and desires assessment,
    26–28
  overview, 9, 37
  reviewing and revising, 27–28,
    30–31
  short-, medium-, and long-term,
    29–30, 32–33, 108
  wealth agenda, 107–8
  writing down, 35
  See also dreams and desires
gold, 150
Goldie, Daniel C., 139
Goldman Sachs, 120
government securities
  bond market as low correlation
    to, 58–59
  risk associated with, 70
  for steady income, 56, 62
  TIPS, 152
  US and world government bond
    indexes, 59
greed/fear cycle, 99–101, 102, 104
greed leading to market plunge, 6, 116

H

"Hank's Banks"
  author selling plan to her clients,
    129–34
  bank renegotiating the deal,
    134–35
  Buffett's bailout, 122–23
  designing a financial product,
    126–29
  financial crises, 122
  investment bank to commercial
    bank conversions, 122–24
  investment opportunity, 124–25
  Paulson's saving of, 119
Hayek, F. A., 147
hopium (foolish hope), 33–34, 35
housing bubble (1998–2007), 40–42
housing bubble burst (2007), 1

I

Iceland bankruptcy, 120
inflation, 66, 70, 153
Inflation Primer, An (Palyi), 139
Inflation Protected Securities (IPS),
    153
inflation risk, 70
information sources for investment
    planning, 43–44, 138–40
insider knowledge, 101–2
interest
    CD interest rates, 40–41, 69
    on financial product for "Hank's
        Bank," 128–29
    as hedge against equity volatility,
        62
    as steady income, 50, 56
    TIPS, 152
interest-rate risk, 59, 70, 151–52
Investment Answer, The (Goldie and
    Murry), 139
investment bankers, 120
investment banks, 121–24
investment planning, 39–72
    asset allocation, 54–57, 105–7
    client enjoys playing the market,
        64–65
    diversification, 53, 54, 57–61,
        106–7, 143–44
    "drip" philosophy, 50, 62–63,
        140–42
    enacting the plan, 89–90
    goals and, 65–69
    overview, 4–5, 72, 104
    portfolio design, 52–54, 104,
        106–7
    qualifications for making
        decisions, 22–23, 101
    resources, 43–44, 138–40
    and risk averseness, 67–71
    strategic alterations, 91–92
    timing the market, 63–65, 101,
        102
    See also assessing your plan;
        commitment to your plan;
        financial advisor; flexibility
investment pornography, 63, 102
investors, types of, 5

IPS (Inflation Protected Securities),
    153

J

JP Morgan Chase, 117, 121

K

kiting, 123
Knight Capital, 136

L

large-capitalization stocks, 60–61
Lehman Brothers, 116–17
LIBOR rate fixing, 136
low correlation investments, 57–58, 60

M

Malkiel, Burton G., 138
market risk, 70
markets
    and adjustments to investment
        plan, 92
    credit markets and toxic assets, 1,
        3, 40, 116
    efficiency of, 52–53
    free market system, 147–48,
        160–61
    See also stock market
Markowitz, Henry, 52–54
maturity date diversification, 58–59
Maxwell, John, 7
Merrill Lynch
    author's application process,
        74–78
    author's decision to leave, 82
    broker bullpen, 80–82
    diversified investment portfolios
        research, 54
    hiring process, 47–48
    sale to Bank of America, 117, 121
    Series 7 Licensing Examination,
        78–79
Microsoft, 56
mint.com, 20, 139
money market funds breaking the

buck, 117–18
Monte Carlo Simulations, 111–12
Morgan Stanley rescue, 3
Morningstar, Inc., 140
municipal bond funds, 152–53
Murry, Gordon S., 139
mutual commitment meeting, 85,
    88–92. See also commitment to
    your plan
mutual funds
    actively managed vs. value-add,
        109
    for commodities investments,
        149–50
    of Dimensional Fund Advisors,
        23–24, 98, 109–12, 140–42
    for Inflation Protected Securities,
        153
    resources on, 140

N
needs assessment, 26–28

O
obstacles and difficulties, addressing,
    91–92
October 10, 2008, DJIA plunge
    author's response to, 3–4, 33–34,
        119–21
    as Black Swan Event, 115–16
    breaking the buck, 117–18
    factors leading to, 1, 3, 116–17
    hope and opportunities left after,
        6–7
    overview, 39–40
    real estate market, 1, 40–42, 116
organization of financial documents,
    105

P
Palyi, Melchior, 139
Paulson, Henry, Jr. "Hank," 119
personal satisfaction. See dreams and
    desires
Poincaré, Henri, 148

portfolio allocation strategies, 169–70
portfolio design, 52–54, 104, 106–7,
    137, 145
portfolio management. See financial
    advisor
Primary Fund (Reserve Group),
    117–18
principles for financial security, 3–5
Putnam Prime Money Market Fund,
    118

R
Random Walk Down Wall Street, A
    (Malkiel), 138
rating agencies, 141
real estate market
    housing bubble, 40–42
    housing bubble burst, 1, 116
    signs of life, 42
rebalancing your financial plan, 105–7
reports on financial position, 23
research, 34–35, 52, 54, 146
Resolution Trust Corporation, 41
resources for investment planning,
    43–44, 138–40
retail investments, 129
retirees
    asset allocation for, 56
    case study, 31–33
    overview, 6
    retirement stool, 154
Rice, Daniel Austin, 11, 12–13
Rice, Edna Evangeline, 11, 14
risk factor exposure, 53
risks
    acceptance of, 160–61
    awareness of, 52, 55, 70
    and equities, 56–57, 150–51
    inflation risk, 70
    interest-rate risk, 59, 70, 151–52
    market risk, 70
risk tolerance
    and asset allocation, 69–71, 96,
        146
    and equities, 150–51
    risk averseness, 32, 67–71
"run on the bank," 118

S

senior debt, 127
short-term bond durations, 151–52
simulations, 111–12
small-capitalization stocks, 60–61
S&P 500 Index, 59, 102, 103
speculation (timing the market),
    63–65, 101, 102
stagflation, 153
statistical analysis tools, 111–12
stock market
    effects of world events, 137–38
    fear of, and Great Depression,
        67, 88
    as hedge against inflation, 150
    on hot tips, 101
    and insider knowledge, 101–2
    volatility of, 21, 55, 60, 62
    See also equities
style drift, 53
Swedish study of twins, 19

T

Taleb, Nassim Nicholas, 115–16
TARP (Troubled Asset Relief
    Program), 118–19
tax consequences of rebalancing, 107
Temporary Liquidity Guarantee
    Program (TLGP), 128
Texas Premium CDs, 41
360 Degrees of Financial Literacy
    (AICPA), 139
time horizon and market risk, 71
time management, 78–79
timing the market, 63–65, 101, 102
TIPS (Treasury Inflation Protected
    Securities), 152
TLGP (Temporary Liquidity
    Guarantee Program), 128
toxic assets
    and credit markets, 1, 3, 40, 116
    and rating agencies, 141
transaction-driven culture, 83, 84, 87,
    102, 104. See also commission-
    based financial advisor
transaction fees from rebalancing, 107

Treasury Inflation Protected Securities
    (TIPS), 152
Troubled Asset Relief Program
    (TARP), 118–19
Turock, Art, 73
'tweeners, 6, 65–67
twins, Swedish study of, 19

U

utility companies, 62

V

value-add mutual funds, 109
value stocks, 60–61
vision for the future, 29–30
volatility
    drip vs., 62
    effective diversification vs., 53,
        60–61, 144
    portfolio design vs., 52, 67, 107
    of stock market, 21, 55, 60, 62

W

Washington Mutual (WAMU), 121
wealth advisor. See financial advisor
wealth agenda, 107–8
webinars, 137
Wheeler, Dan, 109–10
Wilcox, Glover Brown, 14
    women in transition, 6. See also
        Dorothy

ABOUT THE AUTHOR

A WIDELY RESPECTED leader in the investment advisory industry, Kimberly Foss is the president and founder of Empyrion Wealth Management Inc., a sought-after media source, and she is an accomplished author and speaker.

A forward-thinking thirty-year industry veteran, Kimberly founded Empyrion twenty-four years ago to offer her clients straightforward, unbiased advice free of the inherent conflicts of interest often present in relationships with commission-driven stockbrokers. For more than two decades, she has served her clients as a fiduciary, always putting their interests first. Today, Kimberly brings special expertise and real passion to her work with women in transition, including widows and divorcees; small business owners interested in developing or selling of their company; 'tweeners (boomer clients too young to retire, but too old to begin a new career); and pre- and post-retirees. As a trusted advisor, she helps all her clients make smart decisions with their money, avoid costly market mistakes, and work steadily toward their financial goals.

Kimberly believes that quantitative analysis plus qualitative research equals enlightened wealth management, and her investment approach is guided by a powerful combination of mathematical reasoning tempered with an emotional understanding of her clients' financial needs. Her money management expertise is complemented by her ability to demystify money in her conversations. She has an uncanny ability to use common metaphors and stories to ease the understanding of financial issues clients perceive to be difficult. Kimberly's investment mantra, "Stay diversified; stay the course," can be recited by many of her tenured clientele.

Kimberly's financial expertise and sincere dedication to her clients has been acknowledged time and again. Bloomberg Wealth Manager has named Empyrion Wealth Management Inc. one of the nation's Top Wealth Managers several times, and Kimberly appears frequently on Fox News and *Fox Business*, as well as CNBC's *The Call, Power Lunch*, and *The Kudlow Report*. She has also appeared on the *Today Show* and *Good Morning America* and is a regular guest financial expert on a variety of Northern California news programs. In addition, she regularly contributes to the *Wall Street Journal, Worth Magazine*, and MarketWatch, and is a frequent trusted source for a variety of professional publications, including *Financial Advisor, Financial Planning*, and *Investor's Business Daily*. Kimberly also was chosen to be a contributor to *Secrets of the Wealth Makers: Top Money Managers Reveal Their Investing Wisdom*, written by Michael Lane and published by McGraw-Hill; *Stuff About Money*, written by Craig D. Guillot and published by NOLA; *Dirty Little Secrets: What the Credit Reporting Agencies Won't Tell You* by Jason R. Rich and published by Entrepreneur Press; *Mastering the Mommy Track: Juggling Career and Kids in Uncertain Times*, written by Erin Flynn Jay and published by Business Books; and *Financial Intelligence: Advice, Insight, and Counsel from Worth Magazine's Leading Wealth Advisors and Attorneys*, published by Sandow Media.

Kimberly lives in Roseville, California, with her husband and four children.